IN PRAISE OF NAHUM TATE

IN PRAISE OF NAHUM TATE

Selected Writings

Ric Cheyney

Copyright © 2019 Ric Cheyney
Artwork © 2015 Julie Foley

The moral right of the author has been asserted.

Apart from any fair dealing for the purposes of research or private study, or criticism or review, as permitted under the Copyright, Designs and Patents Act 1988, this publication may only be reproduced, stored or transmitted, in any form or by any means, with the prior permission in writing of the publishers, or in the case of reprographic reproduction in accordance with the terms of licences issued by the Copyright Licensing Agency. Enquiries concerning reproduction outside those terms should be sent to the publishers.

Matador
9 Priory Business Park,
Wistow Road, Kibworth Beauchamp,
Leicestershire. LE8 0RX
Tel: 0116 279 2299
Email: books@troubador.co.uk
Web: www.troubador.co.uk/matador
Twitter: @matadorbooks

ISBN 978 1838590 703

British Library Cataloguing in Publication Data.
A catalogue record for this book is available from the British Library.

Printed and bound by CPI Group (UK) Ltd, Croydon, CR0 4YY
Typeset in 11pt Baskerville by Troubador Publishing Ltd, Leicester, UK

Matador is an imprint of Troubador Publishing Ltd

This book is especially for Raymond and Bobby, my two brothers; one in blood, the other in spirit, and both the best imaginable.

Contents

EGO

Lives In Amber	3
Life Tide	3
Biography	4
Obscurity	5
Profile	6
Episode	8
The (Two) Law(s) Of Separation	10
Late (Sonnet Variant)	11
A Certain Knowledge	12
Leaving This Town	13
Over You	15

FAMILY

Redheart	19
My Stepfather	21
Folded	22
Pavement Panic	24
Not Fair	26
Letter To My Daughter Now Thirty	27
Lessons Of Parenthood	28
Wedding Poem	29
Children	31
Harvey Dog	32

OBSERVATION

Streetlight Coming On	39
Light Times Table	41
Postmodern, Sublunar	42
Awaiting Still Revival	43
Helicopters Around Here	44
Vertigo	45
Old Peg Remembers	46
Sibelius: Symphony Six	47
Train(ers)	48
The Naming Of Prats	49
Concerning Destiny	51

EARTH

Mother Earth Rant	55
The Commonwealth Of Crows	56
Eventually	58
Occluded Crow	60
Colour	62
Gang Of Four	64
Robbed	66
On Patrol	68
Double Take	70
Roadside Funeral	72
Epicure	74
Evolution	76
Not Proper Family	78
Don't Mention The Raven	80
Scarecrow	82
Royal Visit	84
Classic	86
Mind How You Go	88

Hubris and Humility	90
Woodpecker At The Birdtable	91
Geo/Political Rant	92
A Slug Sliced In Two	93

NARRATIVE

Detective, Fiction	97
Doll, Car, Park, Doll.	99
Not Found In The Provinces	101
The Clock Of Real Time	104
Outlaw Heart	115
Grievous	130
In Praise Of Nahum Tate	137
Fisher Of Men	138
From Captive Silly Women	139

PERIODICAL

An Interview With Robin Williamson	153
Sacred Songs Part Three	161
John Moriarty: Christian Visionary	164
Teachering More Betterer	168
How To Play Bomb The Glider	172

SONG

(The Ballad Of) Justin Case	179
The Elysian Fields	181
From Here On In To England	182
Once And Future King	183
Poison Road	184
The Fire This Time	185

Greenwood Ride	186
True Love Always	187
Stand By You	188
Always And Even So	189
The Crow Road	191
The Sleeping Lord	192
Looking To Find Land	193
Leeswood Blues	194
The Oldest War	195
Your Karma Ran Over My Dogma	196
Bloody Red Blues	197
This Beleaguered Foundation	198
(Give Me) Your Winning Smile	199
Broken In Love	200
Rebellion In Heaven	201
Lyric Green	202
Eclipse	203
Willingham Girls	204
Bizarro World	205
Song For Bernadette	206
Fields They Loved	207
Night Song In Sherwood	208
Marian's Farewell	209
Wedding Song	210

AUTHOR'S NOTES AND ACKNOWLEDGEMENTS

Several of my earliest published pieces have been left out of this collection. But I am grateful to every editor who has given space (and the occasional prize) to my contributions over the years, and to these bodies and publications in particular:

Butterfly Conservation
Country Quest
Earth Pathways Calendar
Fairlight Books
Flintshire Festival
Flintshire Volunteer Bureau
Mojo
Momentum
New Musical Express
New Statesman
The Other Sock
Pagan Dawn
Poems
Q
The Spectator
Tales Of Volunteering
Vulture

The **SONG** lyrics in this collection, governed as they are by rhythm as much as meaning, have been edited to remove unnecessary repetition. Rules of grammar and punctuation have been applied as closely as is practicable, but not at the expense of other priorities such as humour, ambiguity, drama etc. They are, essentially, included in this book for reading, and they do not always serve as straightforward song-sheets. If you are actually singing along, however, then truly thou art golden, no matter what.

Not Found In The Provinces is a (very affectionate) parody.

See my website www.woodminster.net for further information.

What we changed
was innocence for innocence.
We knew not the doctrine of ill-doing,
no, nor dreamed that any did.
The Winter's Tale

EGO

LIVES IN AMBER I

LIFE TIDE

We walk the speckled beach,
seeking lumps of amber in the glistening sand.

Each stone, shell, gewgaw
sparkles in cathedral wetness,
hauling twin irises
on winches of sight-line pilgrimage.

Sand grain days are barely noticed.

Fad pebbles distract.

But amber, precious and rare,
is the hope and high prize,
a mermaid whisper in the cleansing tide.

LIVES IN AMBER II

BIOGRAPHY

He flew turtles for a living off the coast of Arkansas.
By the batterylight outhouses the cattle-plated orienteering took place,
often causing mild peristalsis of the opal chords
in angelic subcutaneous banter as a result.

He tipped his wing to hazard
like a harper pulling fingers from a string.

One night, over Jerusalem Beach,
his calibrated toe-punch was partially occluded
and he knew his armadillo days were over.

He sank his altercation in a clerkenware store,
totalling the crystals long into the curfew bay.

Occasional sparrowmaids flattered by for circuitry
but nothing breezed his caution
and every invitation was his first.

His final glades were found shimmering in amber,
sunlight still dancing across the vapour trails of memory.

LIVES IN AMBER III

OBSCURITY

She was the southpaw of her clan,
the first to journey, in the teeth of God's apathy,
townward from ways of ancient amber.

Maiden at the square of four,
she coat-tailed daily the rumbling bus,
angling up shy-boy dreams
in thigh-binding skirts,
heel-spark steps on pavement stone,
early arrival
and opening up on time.

Good morning every morning
to stockroom, counter, staff and stair,
her youngtime paid to learn a world
that quickly passed away,
absorbing her efforts entire until
the glimpse-and-turn ambush,
lunch-break recognition
of her grail future in a dusty junkshop window,
forever out of reach,
like a dragonfly fragment
suspended in yellowed resin.

LIVES IN AMBER IV

PROFILE

A child of lack rose from a limited pride
gifted with an occult soul.

Nearby consensus gave him madness,
exiled from genteel entangling.

The metropolis claimed him
like a pinball in flippering streets.

On dancehall legs he dazzled,
psalms of enchantment seeping upward
from his hope-filled mouth.
Camera storms embraced him
in the landslide goldrush grumblings of fame.

Adventure called him through commercial glass.
Tactile confirmation launched his craft.
Sequestered in distant fields, the apprentice laboured on until
all doubt deserted.

Now attention and response were oxygen.
But the clown shadow in his spirit
made wisdom an alien planet.
He agitated galaxies just because he could
while trickles of pine sap approached unseen.

    Husked by time his days became
    A giant empty ambered name
   Whose bleaching light his shadow shape
     Now can not escape.

EPISODE

When sorrow held my head under water
I pretended to be drowned
in hope he'd take the pressure off
and let my soul escape

but no go, Joe:
moustachio'd Lothario
(with too familiar face),
he gripped my neck and pushed down harder.

And he tied me to the railway line,
there to wait and watch my doom,
me too frazzled to question
why he'd not just run me through
with a spike.

Why such grotesque elaboration?
I (never) asked,
as my skull edged toward the buzzing saw.

Still, though, he did club me with a mallet
as the steam train thundered up,
and fiend-like shoved me
at the gashing, splitting blade.

I didn't pretend to be dead on the line, though,
and I faked no slump by the whirring saw.
I had to do something
so struggled to my dying breath.

And even in the drowning brook
my lungs convulsed
and forced me into grappling Mister Grim,
whose leering face I knew so well.

And lo! Arising from water,
bursting my bonds,
twisting free on the sawbench,
emergent under dappled green boughs
below blue sky,
I ambled in the greenwood glades,
that grasping nemesis at my heels no more,
but him still there before me
in the mirror.

THE (TWO) LAW(S) OF SEPARATION

The first dream of the anxious parent
is a nightmare that crunches bones
with grinding claws and spiky teeth.
It replays endlessly in the doom factory of the mind,
phoenixed up when each fell risk
blocks the flow of love's delight
and it is this:
I stumble from the nursery door
in choking grief and shadowed air,
the child asleep for ever more,
torn from my grasp and tender care.

The second dream plays just once
in the cinema of existential consciousness.
It puts all other fears to bed
and leaves them snoring fitfully on warm blue pillows,
carving instead from the mind's dark marble,
a fixéd set of statues
which runs thus:
My darling boy with tender care, polite
and sweetly smiling, tiptoes from my room,
bestows on me a warmly wished goodnight
and leaves me here in winter's growing gloom.

LATE (sonnet variant)

If three score years and ten are mine by right
And spread across a single working day
From six a.m. to midnight, next birthday
I shall be just past nine o'clock at night.
And nine was early days at twenty-one:
My coat just being taken at the door,
The party set to rage till three or four
With bags of time for revelry and fun.
But now I'm pushing sixty and instead,
When I hear music from the street below,
I draw the curtains. In an hour or so
I'll climb the stairs and take a book to bed.
When midnight chimes my lamp may still burn on
But I shall not be reading, I'll be gone.

A CERTAIN KNOWLEDGE

Somewhere between June and August
I lost you
the way a dreamer loses altitude:
inexplicably.

I took to sleeping lunchtimes,
wearied with excitement,
waiting,
while you were busy waving,
gone already.

A secret amputee, I was
unknowingly remote
and well into October I
retained a certain feeling,
perverse against my knowing
that you really were not
coming back.

My knowledge now is certain,
though still in search of sense;
if more precise,
unhelpful none the less.

I lost you in July.

LEAVING THIS TOWN

Bramble Lane, soaked by a thunderous morning,
waits to snag my clothes and lacerate my face.

I am no explorer.
My planned pioneer trail has been blocked
by a landslide of parochial drabness.
Now what?

I'm leaving anyway.
Goodbye to Bramble Lane and its sullen puddles.
Farewell, town of my beginning.
School saw me go last summer;
now not even common sense can moderate my steps.

There are houses on Church Street,
some armed with friends who police an affectionate prison,
and raw new memories on Park Avenue.

I stride past them all.
Bike rides to the frontier,
the maybes of childhood,
light younger eyes now.

At the crossroads my path turns a quarter of the compass
to the more established route of Station Road,
still hunched and flinching from the weather
until the brittle warmth of a grubby carriage
affords me shelter.

Stasis descends like a threat.
Doors clump, calm as prison locks.
Now what?

Existence narrows to a bubble of silence.

The waiting room jerks,
the bookstall creeps away.
Platform, bridge and crossing slide unsteadily by,
then a handful of damp streets.

Just before the fields sweep in,
one last clip of recognition:
Bramble Lane, empty and rebarbative as ever,
sneers an acknowledgement.

OVER YOU

Sunrise happens amid brain-hurt,
revealing how her many sweet utterances
ghost extendedly through your redundant longing.

Sleep quits her for surface repair.
She savours the hour calmly, beyond your loss.

Desire and denial betray you in secret,
blunting her perambulations,
ignoring her pronouncements.
You plan your reconstruction in the ruins of your own home town.

Her countenance is empty
despite her gentled weeping
which is not for you,
not for anyone.

FAMILY

REDHEART

Our cat has brought in a live robin.

Under the kitchen table,
in a chaos of chair legs
where none can see or intervene,
her gentle brutality appals.

Squawks and fluttering punctuate.
Cruelly, expertly,
the warm-fronted herald of winter cheer
is having its life prolonged.

I am a child again.
Screened off by loving arms and slamming doors,
Dad kicks furniture,
punches my fluttering brother,
blacks my squawking sister's eye.
Chairs are scraped, wielded, broken.
Voices challenge, warn, wail,
all made worse by not seeing.
Stop now. Please just stop.

In the crime-scene mystery of afterwards:
a tiny spray of blood on a wall,
blood at my brother's loving eye
the warm bright red of a robin.
Dad has gone but
he'll be back
and always my dad.

Sometimes, we know now,
the worst thing you can do to a robin
is keep it alive.

MY STEPFATHER

Planting potatoes is a political act.

My geography project is due on Monday.
Modern Agriculture And The Environment
enslaves my weekend with a tame surmise
(silent upon a desk in the kitchen).

But I must plant potatoes, he insists,
empowered by economics and the law.

'You can't eat *books*,' he says, chewing my future.
'No booklearnin' till these fields is done.'

His scabby hands demonstrate.
The soft, vulnerable seed rests in rich fenland soil,
fibrous futures protuberant.
They are *his* future: a promise of profit.

I look up from the earth to the man.
His patched gabardine and bitter eyes expose him.
He's just a farmer,
enslaved by systems
that pinch out much feeling.

I tell him we are brothers of a kind:
his harvest will sustain my teenage body,
my books may yet restore his withered soul.

We look at each other with a mild surprise,
silent upon a field East Anglian.

FOLDED

After the polite savageries of lawyers
the children are allowed to visit.

My strong responsible daughter guards her eyes,
tightwire alert in a hesitant hug at the station,
but the bubble-haired boy is awash with cuddles amidships.

We shop for groceries on the way home,
a comforting echo of old routines.

Potato waffles! No nutritional value
but can add bounce to the suffering soul.
The eight-pack is a half-price special.
Shall we?

Trained to police unhealthy indulgence,
sister consents on a cliff edge, radar sweeping,
but brother is all freckled warmth.
Processed food and outmoded mathematics spring the trap.
'Yes! That's *two each*!'

A venn diagram of crumpled tenderness
folds us in silence
for two stretched seconds,
then sister hisses whispers of strangled reprimand:
'No it *isn't*!'

A year ago she'd have added, '*Stew*-ped!'
and he'd have felt no sting.
But we're a broken group now:
you can't be hurting *and* stew-ped.

Strong responsible sisters
understand the law
even as they apply it.
No courtroom required.

PAVEMENT PANIC

My aged mother stands atop the dizzying kerbstone,
confidence fled like a punctured lung,
reaching wordless through vortexing fear
to me. I must catch her,
hold her arms, steady her windblown ship.

She has been fine all morning:
to the car in the wheelchair
then touring the level precinct on foot,
she has rambled like a little girl,
chirruping with shopkeepers,
staring at strange fashions,
whispering clipped critiques.

But now, sudden, on a three-inch cliff,
she earthquakes dumbly,
her stick falls sideways redundant
and only I can save her.

How has this happened?
Time has flipped us in a loop,
swapped us pawn for queen,
sent frailty and seniority spinning
like gulls in a clifftop gale.

How often has she been my rescue:
caught me collapsing mid-toddle
on the precipice of the living-room floor,
cuddled cool the heatful hurt of the day?

Crisis calmed, seated in the café,
I reach across,
cut her lunch into easy morsels
and wonder how soon
my daughter will do the same for me.

NOT FAIR

In the few months since it became my property,
my mother's ancient barometer
has stayed tilted between change and rain,
as if the sun went with her
when she left.

Squalls, glooms and brief respites
have been all my weather,
and now in early summer
I look for a first arising of brightness.

Rain, Change, Fair, still the three sections
attend the mercurial needle like rival suitors,
one firmly out of favour,
while I too am stuck
in sorrowed possession.

I am troubled by this instrument's famed reliability.
Packed and transported from the wake,
it has quickly settled
back to coping easily
with pressure.

I tap the glass.
The needle edges rainward.

LETTER TO MY DAUGHTER NOW THIRTY

Darling,

have you noticed
how childish a word is 'grown-up'?

Grown up is what you have done.

Adults do adultery, adulterating,
queering the lives they've constructed.
Grown-ups groan on and moan on.

Although I know there have been times
when I have not lived up to parenthood
as much as we both may have wished,
you have outshone all our great hopes
comfortably.

You are more grown up than I shall ever be.

Before I close let me just say this
in tribute to your up-growing
and in grateful thanks for the privilege
of having been your dad:

When I was fourteen I pictured a daughter.
She was YOU.

LESSONS OF PARENTHOOD

My daughter has a boy
busy teaching her
all the ache-brained
broken-hurted lessons
she at his age taught me:

There goes youth (you won't miss it).
Time is more relative than Einstein ever imagined.

There is romance,
and then there is real love.

There is exhaustion,
and then there is parenthood.

Having vomit on your chest
can be strangely pleasing.

Sleep, work, disposable income, sanity,
all can be friends you've lost touch with.

And joy, all joy.
Deep bright eruptions
in every Columbus moment.

WEDDING POEM

Where do the games of summer go?
Onward, down the dappled lanes
of boyhood's questing tomorrow,
spun like loops of wooden trains

which only catch parental feet.
Thus my fleetfoot boy skips out
to taste the rain and feel the heat,
eyes on fire and void of doubt.

In Parentworld the wooden train
is strewn across the carpet town.
I step inside a circled plain
(so wooden bridges don't fall down)

en route to open wide the door
which chimes, announcing she whose ways
will charm him from the Toytown floor,
catch his heart in nets and stays

of living love and loving life.
The gentle snare of young romance
will see him go to take a wife
with one brief, backward, grateful glance.

Behold the sin of manful pride
that none will ask (and none can say
against the father of the bride)
why no one gives the *groom* away.

Where do the games of summer go?
Packed away like wooden trains
when clocks are ticking childhood slow,
scattered down the questing lanes.

We pack the Toytown tracks away
not guessing it's the final time,
not doubting we'll be back next day
nor frightened by the doorbell chime.

CHILDREN

From whelk-sop decrepitude they rise,
clanging any old tin boxes
to the tune of subversive beatitudes.

Skittled into receptiontide their mixturing scuffles and sparks,
though every captured camp is gone by morning.

You assumed initial ownership,
but a polaroid timescale flipped you like stunt doubles,
splintering disruption in your face,
the reins tugging emergently over the horsehead nebula neck.

Now behold:
high-chair diplomacy and storybook bartering
are your only tokens of managed surrender.
They have trained you to welcome your own expulsion
from the shifting, shaking, field of play.

HARVEY DOG

Sorry this is a long story, but if you are interested in SOUL or SPIRIT, you might want to read on.

This is the story of HARVEY. He was Bee's dog when I first got to know her. I've never been a dog person, and Harvey felt the same about me when I first appeared on the scene. On my first visit to Bee's home, Harvey got me alone in the bedroom, slammed the door shut and gave me a thorough talking-to, not just about his role as Bee's companion-protector but also explaining how anyone hoping to hurt, trick or abuse her could be guaranteed a thorough savaging by the canine version of Death-And-Hell's-Despite. This was, of course, all delivered in a window-rattling, booming voice that left room for neither doubt nor interruption. I understood his motives and appreciated his concern whilst naturally resenting his abrupt, hectoring mistrust, but within a few weeks we had developed quite a warm and comforting relationship. We were, after all, both devoted to Bee.

Usually Bee and I would walk Harvey together, but occasionally he and I would walk in Prestwich Clough just as a twosome. Very often we would find a golf ball by a pathside. I would throw it and Harvey would chase it down and... *keep* it. He just never got the idea of *returning* the ball for another go. Staunch Cancerian like me, he had a keen awareness of property and ownership.

As I say, I'd never been a dog person, never loved a dog, so you can bet Harvey must've been one heckuva good one for me to love him the way I did. There was certainly a lot to love.

Along with actual reasoning intelligence (oh yes) and his aforementioned communication skills, he was modest, playful and athletic. He had a trick of scurrying through tall grass, leaping above it and then just freeze-framing himself in mid air for a classic 'action shot', half high-jumper half ballet dancer.

He also had the keenest sense of responsibility. The first time we did the clough without Bee, he lost me, or thought he did. In fact I had lost him, just by turning early off the usual path and being hidden by trees. I saw his mildly concerned trot back to the house to check, then a brindled streak as he zoomed past in the other direction, an expression of abject, serious worry on his face as he raced to find where I could have gone missing. Let's just stop here for a moment and check for sentimental embroidery, shall we? He *zoomed* by, visible only in profile and for less than a second, and not even close up: could I *really* see and read the expression on his face? Well, of course there was a considerable amount of body language involved, but I promise you his face was dark with concern.

He had quite broad shoulders, and he needed them for all the burdens he had to bear and the alertness he had to show on behalf of all the family. On occasions the petrol-powered lawnmower would sputter and fail to start. Every time, without fail, Harvey would leap at it and bark his loudest to protect us from whatever predator was making that roaring noise.

Another of Harvey's fine qualities was his discernment when reading and evaluating character. Sitting in the front room where he could see them, or in the hall where he couldn't, Harvey let most passersby pass by without comment or suspicion, but every so often he would raise his head and bluster gently to warn us that 'riff-raff' were in the neighbourhood again. Invariably a quick glance outside would confirm his assessment. What a darling he was.

When he developed serious epilepsy, he was distraught to be incontinent, stinking like the devil's own toilet and in the grip of horrific shakes. In these episodes I would cuddle him on Bee's bed and assure him that even though he was piddling all over us, he was still a "Good boy!" It wasn't even a white lie.

Pretty soon, however, the fits became full-time permanent seizures, and the vet had to grant him full-time permanent relief. That was in 2008.

Harvey has been sending me golf balls ever since. I've found them in obscure, impossible, ridiculous places, and in logic-defying circumstances. It's as if he's found himself in Heaven (where of course he belongs) and Oh, he gets it now: bringing the ball back, *that's* what he should have been doing all those times. So he's bringing them all back now. I've literally lost count of the golf balls he's brought me but it's well into the thirties. And I found another one today. In the middle of a path I've been mowing and clearing for *years*, there it was, well settled in, one third of it below ground level.

Every cell in my brain says when you die, that's the end and nothing follows. But these golf balls keep coming; and please note that it's never Bee who finds them: the golf ball was something Harvey enjoyed with *me*, not us, and it's *I* who keep finding them, in the garden, on the Wilmslow 10k run, under the car etc. On a walk near Loggerheads Park I found one in the bare middle of a path I had walked down just a few *seconds* earlier. They are always *individual* finds too, except for one occasion when two showed up in different parts of the garden on the same afternoon; they were different makes, but both had the number 2 on them; spooky, huh?

I can imagine rational explanations for nearly all of these events (although several of the garden finds seem to have emerged as if spat out by the ground). But I like to think dear Harvey is still looking out for us. Maybe the lawnmower no longer growls in my direction, and the riff-raff don't stroll by his territory anymore, but our beloved and noble companion has found a way to continue voicing his support. Thank you, darling Harvey, our much missed *good boy*.

If you're grieving the loss of anyone, keep an open mind and look out for the signs and connections. You never know what might turn up.

OBSERVATION

STREETLIGHT COMING ON

It flicks on where an instant before was nothing
and, dim enough already,
dims further on that instant
as if mere arrival were all of life,
as it is all of light.

Then begins the struggle:
the several and diverse faltering moments before
the hold on life is secured;
and even so
the power is not evident at present:
this life must wait for darkness to magnify its station.

What little life, and pointless, it holds:
arbitrary, almost adrift on its pedestal
till blue evening deepens to black night.

Then behold its dominance of context:
how clear the sphere of gold in night's deep darkness;
how welcome that warmth to wayward strangers
ghosting by below.
How startled are the stars by its outshining;
how bravely it signals out to others at dark distances.

Then are we all
glad of that sure goodness which is light,
cheered when bright maturity
survives those yellow, frail, first flickerings
our shadows to dispel.

And if later we see its glow betrayed by time,
exposed, redundant in the modern morning,
well, what of that?
We fear no less the darkness then,
we love no less the light.

Child,
on life's arrival,
claim that light.
Struggle in starting
if struggle you must,
but hoard that light for blazing in the shadows, and,
when your time of brightness comes,
shine;
end thrift, reach out and burn
as each in his own darkness has need of you.

LIGHT TIMES TABLE

Star dappled darkness.
Candle romance devotional.
Lamp dogged hopeful in the storm.
Fire companion caves and shadows.
Moon changing earth, tides and seas.
Head mirror dazzle.
Lime attention central.
Fluorescent supermarket bright clean.
Arc fierce fusion.
Day gold standard.
Flood public combat arena.
Sun life hope growing. Star.

POSTMODERN, SUBLUNAR

Sublunar, postmodern,
funny is quick,
sad slow dead.
Gravity lifts dull to glory,
levity sinks bright to banal.
The mass echoes in ancient churches,
the masses bawl on fleeting screen.
Games are studied like gnostic text,
wars played out redacted.
Listen:
commentators turn golf to earthquake,
tsunamis sound like village cricket.
Lucky we whose tempests are goalless draws,
leaving slaughters eclipsed
the way our cold satellite
can shadow the raging sun.

AWAITING STILL REVIVAL

Here in the west the Welsh are trolls:
short, swarthy, black thatched,
Gallic, bitter rebukes to foreigners
they could despise but don't.

Here, too, the Welsh are chapel:
flinty, gritty keepers of the gospel glow;
hard, patient, humble,
awaiting still a revival
secular Britain will not countenance.

The occupying air is mocking of spirit
but Wales has not forgotten
the humane hero and the golden soul.

Perhaps the Christ they see is still
the tall, white, slender, longhaired Lord
from nursery bible picture books
when all enlightened scholars know
that Jesus walked this earth a troll,
a squat and rough-haired, swarthy Jew.

Perhaps they see, here in western Wales,
a Christ from colonial fiction that they recognise:
one of their own.

HELICOPTERS AROUND HERE

The yellow mountain rescue is old, heavy, slow,
but she rotors a thin high frequency,
the swish whisper of a spy in church.
Viewless through trees and ridges
she is known by her patient swooping,
slow meanderings gently alert for waving hands.

The red air ambulance is lighter, thinner, flatter,
but thunders her blades darkly,
echoing rock on rock
like a mad robot woodcutter
thwacking angrily at one stubborn block.
There is grim autocracy in her descent,
the strained, private silence
then restart louder than before.

Yellow's departure is a happy ending:
back to base and warmth restored.

Red lifts away with still our hopes attaching,
tilting in volatile currents,
uncertainty late arriving,
the future rocking in the balance.

VERTIGO

Every ascent is hacked from rock,
each cragged hard narrow ledge gained earned.
We dare, teeter, suffer cold, shock,
imbalance, striving, conquering
but triumph cut, so well we've learned
each aching stage craves plummeting,

because below is not distance,
only time; a single wire strain,
just one cramped truce with patient chance
will cast us back not to cold stone
but arid, empty, bald flat plain,
no summit reached and all hope gone.

Public voices spurn such failures;
urge, galvanize, spew rhetoric,
point at glimpsed, not reached futures
calm and airily placed, nestled
atop ranges so heroic:
brave eagles' wings folded, settled.

But secret hearts rebel, glance round.
Abandoned stages of the climb
eclipse escarpments not yet found.
Memories, though jeering mobs condemn,
drop, sheer, down the cliff face of time
like lost coins, and we go with them.

OLD PEG REMEMBERS

Until that rude enslavement all my days
had been a schoolboy's Friday homeward rove.
My heart knew not the pangs of time or love.
Pirene's fountain dappled where I'd graze.
The jewelled bridle, swung in occult ways,
rough tugged my tongue, strapped sharp my eyes above
the bolting miles I sunward kicked and strove.
Why is it now Bellerophon I praise?
My yielding has no gloss of how or why.
Perhaps I learned of loneliness that day,
or thrills of shared endeavour? Anyway,
to slay Chimaeras one must fight and fly.
For cherished slaves the lonely free live worse.
Enigma saddles every broken horse.

SIBELIUS: Symphony Six

Allegro molto moderato starts in the title, an endlessness of ess:
slow sliding snow slopes, sorrowful,
eyes to the horizon: mountains and sky.
Then skid-busy sleighride up fell and glide dell.
How to be happy in a minor key.

Allegretto moderato is a snowscape.
High-stepping snow-shoes, Disney on stilts.
Ice Queen enchantment under the rime,
pantomime villain in standard time.
War waits just beyond the horizon. Readiness is all.
Tooting ships across the sound, pitching waves of farewell.

Poco vivace is a lot more poco than vivace.
Gathering armies numb skull march,
fighting for families far from home, down fell and frost fall.

Allegro molto wears a statesman's suit:
the acceptable face of freezing grief.
Homeward with stories sad to tell
of how we kept a candle burning in the dark;
how the body froze but the heart warmed on,
clinging to the ledge with ice tipped fingers.
The end of ess: steps down lines of loss,
marching home to the march past;
quiet reflection in Remembrance Garden:
bright red seepage into springtime colours
sorrowed with snow.

TRAIN(ERS)

I'm riding the train
And standing beside
A wheelchairéd boy
Whose witheréd legs
Will never propel
Him ever again
If ever they did.
But someone he trusts
Has let him be dressed
With bright new running shoes, dazzling pristine on his toy feet.

You might as well hand him a bike.

What would *you* do, given the choice:
continue the fiction,
scuff them up,
send him out with fake aged footwear?
Or close the book on childhood stories,
salt-rinse his cuts,
confess that running is among
the things he's never done?

THE NAMING OF PRATS

Shane, Wayne and Dwayne
were the names that guaranteed strife
when I started as a teacher,
but things have moved on since.

Now it can be anything
except an actual name
or a proper spelling.

So it's Cevin with a 'c' and Tayler with an 'e',
Airun, seriously,
and we haven't even started on the girls.

Brookelin and Madyson,
conceived during the CSI NY ad break.
Chlamydia, oh that's pretty.
It can only be a matter of time.

Drop-dead gormless Lowleeta
with the nails, hair, skirt and *skin*
of a middle aged madam,
what is that you are chewing, a *football?*
Put it in the bin.

Terry Bull, are you *sure?*
I remember the good old days
when Trouble was only his *middle* name.
His sister, Aimee Isadora Bull, not.

Now, careful as you're leaving.
Don't disturb Angel and Buffy,
the goth despairadoes.
Dyed black hair, powder white faces,
ebony lipstick, nail varnish and earrings.
And we haven't even *started* on the girls.

CONCERNING DESTINY

Is destiny created
or printed like a ticket at your birth,
permitting certain journeys
within the transport system of the earth?

Does every caterpillar,
upgrading from Economy to First,
forget its former status
the moment that the pupa starts to burst?

There came a man from Tarsus,
mistaken in the spelling of his name
but, turning at the crossroad,
he'd always been the Saint that he became.

John Lennon left nativity
behind and broke his stick of rock in two,
belatedly revealing
NEW YORKER clearly stamped the full length through.

Thus Churchill stayed a Tory
regardless of the stripe of his elector,
T S Eliot was English
and Hitchcock was a Hollywood director.

EARTH

MOTHER EARTH RANT

Beware the sentimentalist who gushes about 'the beauty of Mother Nature'. If Nature was a Mother she would not have produced the cuckoo; she would not have produced man. People who talk of the beauty of Nature often seem to forget that man is a wild animal. They think a dormouse is cute and a redwood is magnificent, so Nature must be beautiful. They forget the brain-eating parasites and the hideous viruses. I know Nature *can* be beautiful, but its energies are generally yin and yang, male and female, dark and light.

I do, however, recognise the concept of Mother Earth. This planet (with help from the rest of the universe, aka Father Sky) gave birth to us all. Earth certainly has beauty, though sometimes of a dark and frightening kind. Part of that beauty comes from her fragility, and from the thought that she is rare, possibly unique.

Just as Nature oscillates between rampant domination and bare survival, Earth's energies can produce casual destruction (volcanoes, earthquakes) and gossamer vibrations (hummingbirds and butterflies). Her fault, if she has one, is an excess of generosity.

I am often brought low by my base nature, but Mother Earth, in all her beauteous creativity, is what I strive to live up to.

THE COMMONWEALTH OF CROWS

(sixteen ways of looking at a black bird)

ARTWORK BY

JULIE FOLEY

EVENTUALLY

A long time ago,
by the purest accident,
all strains of earthy creatures,
gravity bound, lumpen, proletarian,
reached up freakish limbs,
umbrella-boned mutations
and the like,
hoisted the flag of what comes next?
and, as if by Fortune's charter,
somehow harnessed air.

Thus, eventually,
CROWS!

OCCLUDED CROW

Screened by naked branches,
fragments of crow
(wing flaps and nose cone)
settle mosaically
on fragments of tree
(twigs and bough).

COLOUR

Like the ravishing beauty
whose face requires no make-up,
the crow understands
that there are many shades of black.

GANG OF FOUR

Wind betossed and pitching,
four flustered crows
perch like scouting whalers
on steepled pinetop twigs,
wittering and whingeing,
ganging up wontedly,
grumbling like jaded pensioners
in a drafty nursing home.

ROBBED

How incompetent of the English tongue,
so fond of morphing noun into verb,
to make a fresh infinitive
of crow.

What were they thinking?
Such prodigal waste of noble connection,
clever connotation
and wit by association.

How in God's own name and language
did they ever come to imagine
that a mere cockerel
could crow?

ON PATROL

On days of gentle sunshine
the sky police arrive
in twos, threes
and practised good humour
to steer loitering buzzards down the valley,
escorting them with firm courtesy
off the premises.

No need for any trouble, sir.
No caws for alarm,
ha ha ha.

DOUBLE TAKE

Glimpsed at a distance
in the margin of my zooming windscreen,
a cloud of rooks
vanishes round the corner.

Three seconds later,
framed by my passenger window,
a treeful of motionless Disney crows
blink bewildered innocence
for tourist cameras.

ROADSIDE FUNERAL

A hapless red pheasant
lies prone at the roadside,
pecked and attended
with perfect decorum
by one obsequious sorrowful crow
in dignified charcoal sobriety.

There are no other mourners.

EPICURE

Lamb eyes are a delicacy
to crows.

As the noble, ungainly lobster
is boiled alive by humans,
so the livid embodiment of youngness
is blinded by corvid cruelty.

I have not witnessed these atrocities
and cling to the hope that neither is true.

EVOLUTION

From much digging in the ground
the rook now has no feathers at its beak.
Let this be a lesson to all crows.

NOT PROPER FAMILY

Jays fire nasty gripes at each other,
spiteful blares of carping fishwifery.

Magpies are murderous thugs
with football rattle voices in the morning.

Mister Jackdaw is a prim, respectable,
wife-beating braggart.

These could never be crows.

DON'T MENTION THE RAVEN

Hacks label her a raven-haired beauty,
but ravens have feathers, not hair.
Do not stir up trouble.

SCARECROW

A broomstick-skeletoned bumpkin
stands idly exposed
at fieldscape centre,
pestered by a hot dry breeze.

His rigid arms mock boasting anglers
but are themselves adorned
by thick, stretched, subversive epaulettes
of crow dung.

ROYAL VISIT

I am dodging this crow
the way I dodge my children:
for the joy of travel to planet other.

I skulk by the gate like a paparazzo.

Her lustrous lacquered gloss
balances on the garden bench
too big and strange for the territory,
like an ebony Vulcan bomber
trundling round a council car park.

She parachutes awkwardly down
to wish the lesser celandines and clovers a good morning
and ask them what they do.

When she pivots in situ
her dexter eye impales me.

The visit concludes abrupt.
She climbs importantly skyward
and limousines away to the wuthery wood.

CLASSIC

In air as on land
there is an old straight track.

Witness the simple profundity
of crow flight.

MIND HOW YOU GO

A fierce wind buffets the road,
scattering crows like tattered rags
against the leaden milk of sky.

They are flung sideways out of the fields,
across the blustered highway,
into the hazard of traffic.

Take care.

HUBRIS AND HUMILITY

Human pride is always riding for a fall. We have called ourselves the Crown Of Creation, the dominant species, the top of the food chain, but life-forms ranging from microscopic viruses to planet-hugging mushrooms could challenge that perceived supremacy. And sometimes Mother Earth herself steps in to remind us that she will be around long after she has buried every boast.

If a category-five storm tours your neighbourhood slowly enough, you will acquire true humility. The sea, as any lifeboat volunteer will tell you, does not even know your name. And the powers that keep everything spinning, well, they cannot be properly imagined.

The tsunami that wrecked the Fukushima nuclear power plant was triggered by an earthquake that knocked our home planet four inches off her own axis. It shortened the distance between Japan and the USA by eight whole feet.

She is Mother Earth. Don't mess with her. Instead, get out there, grab a lungful of clean fresh air, give humble thanks, and marvel at her magnificence.

WOODPECKER AT THE BIRDTABLE

She's too tall,
clings to the roof in puzzled lateral trapeze mode.
I've seen them skinhead hard with scarlet mohicans
pecking hell out of peanuts
but she's an old hippie with rust patches,
dowdy in shabby tat
and tired sixties polka-dot panels.
Why come at all? It's summer:
a few hard crusts are her best hope here.

She drops curious to the flooring,
inspects the gable,
appears ready to powerdrill the corner.
Hey, lady, that's planed pine.
Do a lotta spliffs as a chick, didya?

But no. She stoops, steps trepid under the lintel,
picks a crumb with micrometer beak,
holds it, stoned scientist, *ages*,
then snaffles.

Finally, scared off by nothing,
she does the routine miracle
back to the trees.

GEO/POLITICAL RANT

Like the apocryphal taxi driver when asked for directions to a difficult destination, my first response to a political problem in the UK is invariably, "Well, I wouldn't start from *here*," and this is especially true regarding the issue of land ownership.

The evolution of the UK land map is a history of the bullying brutality of feudalism, privilege, enclosure, industrial agriculture and social injustice on a Lex Luthoran scale of criminality. It is so deeply woven into our national dna that even a civil war would probably not resolve it.

But resolve it we must. Current levels of soil erosion indicate that within four generations the UK will see its final harvest, and globally the figures are even worse. We must find a way to winnow out the carpetbaggers, vandals and asset-strippers, and replace them with people who will work in partnership with the land, not against it; people who have a proper sense of commitment and responsibility, of belonging to a place, and the value of that place.

There is, of course, a solution, but even if we were to elect a wise, green government I cannot picture that solution being achieved without massive internal strife. My best hope is that, as the crisis builds, a spreading sense of desperation will prompt us to do the wise green thing.

If your system of government gives the ownership of a thousand acres to one family, and a concrete box to another, that system needs to be changed. I definitely wouldn't want to start from here. But we've got to.

A SLUG SLICED IN TWO

It was accidental, not important.
The quick, calm, sensible shears
were busy settling the wilderness.
The slug was unnoticed;
now it is undone.
It oozes its wound outward,
a silent, slow motion
split spilt cauldron of like guts
that look like pain.
Blue black, jelly, earth brown,
the lesion will grope to infinity,
a complete failure to heal.

Thus now slugs.
They crusade mutely in not well tended gardens,
incommunicado, unco-operative.
Shears work in concert,
tidying doomed remnants
together.
Exposed, which is their vulgar norm,
slugs are all tenderness.
They huddle under infamous weeds,
drawn towards wildness,
to chaos for cover.
Shears are steel,
the blades,
but slugs are lymphatic
like heart.

Now as tempered mechanisms
snick and clack a criss cross
our fenced off land
the fey slime-drenched blob,
single sucker of common vulnerability,
will shudder the more often;
this crude neatening encounter
more frequently repeat.

NARRATIVE

DETECTIVE, FICTION

> *There's an imprint on my window pane*
> *Of a bird that tried to dodge the rain.*
> Bobby Seymore

He lived in a small town a handful of miles from the school. He taught languages; he could speak them. Every break time he would sit in the staff room and pretend to not be looking at her. Colleagues would be puzzled: how come he seems so stupid at break time?

It was because she was there.

She taught humanities: history and geography. He used to wonder how she could cross the room without turning every head.

He began writing to her; secret notes that concealed his identity. The letters told her how beautiful she was. His love was true: it made no demands. He kept his distance for fear of disturbing her. Her husband was the most fortunate of men.

Time passed. She began to perceive clues in the letters. An identity revealed itself, like fingerprints on glass.

Flattered, attracted, she left a secret note of her own, suggesting a time and place. Her husband had long ago forgotten his great fortune.

A time and place; co-ordinates on a map where two roads meet. Alone at the bar she saw a familiar face approaching.

Secrets, veiled references, metaphor. Often more is understood than was ever intended. Chemistry, the quantum leap, the random catalyst, combustion.

At break time in the staff room now the talk is all about the scandal. She has gone, along with her lover, a science teacher. Her husband is devastated, aren't we all?

He joins in now, not pretending. It makes a welcome change from languages.

DOLL, CAR, PARK, DOLL.

When I got to the car park I found a small group of people standing around my car. There were two women, two children and a doll.

The doll was very tall, and soft. Its long legs seemed endless. Its body was long too. Its face was very flat and round. Its long blonde hair was tied in two plaits.

The girl was not quite as tall as the doll, so as she held its ankles up to her face the doll's face brushed the ground.

The boy was taller than the girl. He watched his sister's brutality with mute, calm interest.

The girl began banging the doll's head on the ground. The long blonde plaits clung to the tarmac. Each upward movement left wisps of blonde on the ground.

The doll's face developed a grey shadow in the middle of its bright pink forehead.

The boy took a shiny finger out of his nose and spoke.

"Do you like your doll?"

The girl thought for a moment.

"Yes, of course I do. I love her."

"Why are you banging her head on the ground, then?"

The girl's eyes dashed to the doll's face. For a moment she looked worried, but she shook that off and banged some more.

"She likes it."

The boy had anticipated this petulance, apparently, for his reply was immediate.

"I'll bang *your* head on the ground, then."

The girl looked into her brother's face.

"Blow your nose," she said.

The boy walked carefully around the blonde plaits and stood next to his mother. She was talking to the other woman. She began to play with the boy's hair as she talked.

The girl turned her attention to me. Her gaze was hard to bear.

"That's a beautiful doll," I said. "What's her name?"

"She hasn't got one."

"Really? Oh, poor dolly."

The girl turned the doll right side up and cuddled it. Its face flopped onto her shoulder.

"She's new."

"Yes," I said, "I can see that. Are you going to give her a name?"

The girl's eyes continued looking at me, but they saw something else.

"Yes."

"Oh, good. A doll needs a name."

The girl looked at her mother. It was time to go. I said goodbye and climbed into my car.

Backing out of the parking space, I might have rolled over the wisps, I don't know.

NOT FOUND IN THE PROVINCES

My name does not matter. I do not believe these papers will ever be found. It is not for posterity that I am writing this brief and probably inaccurate account of my endeavours here in this library of dust and pale echoes. My work at the academy, which led me by chance to this place, is now a shadow, the fading memory of a dream.

My study of New Testament heresies was almost complete. Publication, notoriety and a Regius professorship awaited me once a few obscure references had been tracked down. One of these concerned what Estrada, in his *Treatise Of Gnossos* (Cairo, 1924) called the Sect Of Binary Return. Apparently originating in Corinth, this heretical group centred its belief in New Testament references of a numerical and paradoxical nature. They claimed that the soul, after death, undergoes a conversion into two independent states of existence, one absent from earth and corporeal; the other, present but invisible. Among their authorities they cited Saint Paul's assertion that, "the things which are not seen are eternal," (2 Corinthians 4:18) and the risen Christ's statement that he must, "vanish in order to facilitate the arrival of his other." (I use Estrada's own translation of the notorious Binary Scrolls, an incomplete set of manuscripts deposited at that time in the Bodleian but subsequently denounced by Fortier, amongst others, as forgeries, and removed).

My attempts to trace the Binary Scrolls had not long begun when Estrada's notebooks yielded the perplexing reference which, in its inevitable obscurity and eventual confirmation, led me finally and precipitously to my fate.

The notebooks cited only one other account of the sect published prior to Fortier's scandalous involvement. This was an entry in *Handforth's Universal Illustrated Encyclopaedia* (London, 1911) under the heading, "Heresy". I was dismayed but not surprised when the encyclopaedia could not be traced by any of the major university libraries in either the United States or western Europe. The smallest textual controversy can have more victims than any war.

One evening, however, I called in at my local branch library, a building I once treasured for its mixture of grandiose town hall architecture and quiet backwater atmosphere, but which is now both playground and prison to the endless succession of my days.

Unable to find the biography a chance impulse had sent me in for (I wonder now what crossroads of meandering time coaxed me from my homeward walk, and indeed how much or little chance had to do with it), I stopped on my way out at the small section of mahogany shelving given over to "Books For Sale". *Handforth's Universal Illustrated Encyclopaedia* lay on the bottom shelf.

Complete in nine unnumbered volumes, dark red, cloth bound, it was a second edition, dated 1922 (I did not miss the chronological correlation with Estrada's studies).

The library was about to close and I did not have enough money for the whole set, so I bought only the fifth volume, GOLDAU – JYOTISHA. Quickly confirming that it included the reference I sought, I paid the librarian and left.

I returned the next day to buy the remaining volumes. My colleagues would envy my owning a book that did not exist.

What I found in the library did not completely defy logic, but it sent out a fatal challenge to my credulity. The encyclopaedia was still there on the bottom shelf, but it was now complete in *ten* volumes. Instead of a gap where I had made my purchase, there were now two volumes, marked GOLDAU – HOLMFIRTH and HOLM OAK – JYOTISHA. In size both matched the book I had bought the day before.

Believing I knew what would happen if I bought the full set, I took only the two volumes and hurried home, my footsteps on the evening pavements stalked by silent dread.

I compared the texts that night, flicking through the smooth pages in the tangled geometry of dim light provided by my desk lamp and an old illuminated globe once owned by my father. There were no essential differences. The text, pages and illustrations were identical.

The next day, a Thursday, I went again to the library. This time I found my section of the encyclopaedia covered by four volumes. On the lowest shelf of the books for sale I found the fifth, seventh and eighth volumes. They covered GOLDAU – HAMILTON, HOLM OAK – INSECTICIDE and INSECTIVORA – JYOTISHA. Volume six, HAMILTON – HOLMFIRTH, was missing.

Thus my vigil began. I sat at the corner table and waited to see who, if anyone, would return for the other volumes. No one came. When the library closed I hid among the tall lines of shelves as the lights were switched out and the staff went home. When silence and darkness enveloped the library I returned to my table to wait.

I have been here ever since. No one has come to reopen the library which is now grey with dust. The gallery and upper offices remain locked. Sometimes I climb the stone steps to the balcony and survey the angled lines of shelving, the marbled pillars, the domed ceiling, the recesses which hold the small specialised collections. In the half-light of late afternoons I sometimes hear footsteps echo among the shelves, but see no one.

Using other reference books I have begun work assembling the missing volume, knowing it is all there in my study at home. I have completed less than half the entries but already it exceeds the length of the original.

THE CLOCK OF REAL TIME

THE HOUR

My job is simple. I have to embroider the flag. Every day I come here from the village to earn our ethnic improvement grant. I sit here in the dust and sew the tiny threads which will make up, one day, the glory of the new flag.

Paco, my husband, says it is like laying hairs over the ocean, because the threads are so tiny and the flag is so big. It began as just plain white cloth but now part of it is green. I do not have the pattern. The Generals send a messenger each month. He reports back on my progress, and twice now they have delivered orders for the next section to be started. It has been all green so far, but I was told when I began that there will be blue and yellow later, and white. The white won't just be left; that will have to be embroidered too. There won't be any red. I asked.

The orders come in thick soft envelopes sealed with dark red wax stamped with the government crest. A cavalry officer opens them and hands them to the messenger, who tells me what they say. It is very grand when the officer holds out the orders, his long glove covered in the dust of four days riding. When the messenger has explained, he gives the orders back to the officer. Then the officer clicks his heels and salutes in a very grand manner, and rides back into the territory. Paco likes to watch all this from the steps of the clock museum.

Paco has been the museum attendant all his life, since he was seven. It used to be a shop in the frontier days. It is still made of the same wood the first owner built it with, although the rest of the town is made of steel and glass and concrete now. We are in the middle of Main Street, but that name comes from the old days. In fact we are on the outskirts of the town. I can sit in the street all day without a rider passing by, and most of what we can see from the front is the territory.

I have never been into the museum. Paco says it is two rooms; the first one is filled with ticking which will drive you mad, and the second is filled with the silence of the clock of real time. That silence will drive you mad too, Paco says, unless you are meant to be there. It is Paco's job to find out if you are meant to be there, by asking the pendulum question.

People do not visit the museum much. Paco says it is an evil place. He says a clock should tell the time for a reason, not just because it's a clock. He says the time in the room is wasted time, because nobody is wanting to know the time in there. And for Paco, it is a bad thing to waste time. I tell him he is wasting *his* time too then, because he is looking after the clocks for nothing. This makes him angry. But I know it is the clock of real time that makes his job worth doing. He is the guardian and guide to the clock; an important job, even if the pay is no good.

When someone comes to see the clock of real time, Paco has to warn them about it first, and make sure that they should be there. He has to tell them how dangerous it is to consult the clock without good reason, and then he asks them the pendulum question. Then he has to warn them about the clock's face and how to read it. It is not like other clocks. It has two dials and the numbers are turned around so that on the second dial the four is at the top; because that is the top, the middle of your life. Without that warning more people would go mad than they have already. They might think they are near the end of their life when in fact they are only in the middle.

People come from all over the world just to see the clock. Many of them only half believe in it. They think it might be just a story the Indians tell to trick the gringos out of their horses. Or they think it is only the journey that matters. One or two have found it too late.

Paco tries to keep out the ones who will go mad. He says they are the wrong sort. I know our neighbour, Gabriel, thinks Paco is mistaken about that, but I do not know what to think. Maybe it is true what Gabriel says, that there are people who need to know their time before the clock is ready to tell them, even if it casts a shadow on the time they have left. But also maybe they are just what Paco calls them, wielders of words. They can answer the pendulum question because words are a kind of magic that they use, but they are not saying true words.

The question Paco asks is always the same: What must we say to one who offers knowledge? I have heard many answers to it. They are all different. I don't know how Paco can tell when the answer is right. Perhaps he cannot. That might explain the mistakes he has made, although he has made only a few. He says he can tell because the first owner, Harry Jack, gave him the way of understanding the words of men and women.

No, there have not been many women. Paco says it is not a thing a woman always needs to know, but always a man at some time needs to see the clock. Perhaps that is why I have never seen it, but lately I have been thinking I might want to see it one day. I think it has to do with the flag.

QUARTER PAST

Paco likes to tell people the story of how he was given the museum to look after. His eyes crinkle then, because he can tell about Harry Jack from Texas, the man who built the clock store.

It was a general store then. Harry Jack sold blankets to the Indians and food to the townspeople. He adopted Paco when he was four. Paco doesn't remember anything about his life before Harry Jack. Gabriel, our neighbour, *should* remember but he says Paco just arrived one day and stayed, helping Harry Jack. So nobody knows where Paco is from. Maybe he was an Indian. Gabriel can't say; all he can remember is that they found him in the back yard talking to the cockerel.

Paco helped Harry Jack for four years. He helped load and unload wagons for buyers and sellers, and keeping the jars full was his job. Every night Harry Jack would cook dinner in the back room. Paco says Harry Jack was a great cook. His speciality was Mexican food, but he could make everything tasty, and there was always plenty of it.

Harry Jack used to laugh every time he cracked an egg and shout, "Look out below!" When he chopped the pepper he would shout, "Watch out, boys and girls, here come those god damned peppers again!" and roar with laughter. Then he would toss the pepper in the pan and say, "All right, you god damned peppers, here's where you get yours!"

Paco likes to say these things with Harry Jack's voice, the way *he* used to say them. He tells me I should cook with more laughter sometimes, because Harry Jack said cooking with laughter is the best cooking there is, and his cooking always tasted good. Gabriel says cooking always tastes good when you are hungry, which is what Paco and Harry Jack *were* most of the time. But Paco says what does Gabriel know? Nothing, because who can be hungry in a food shop? Then they argue, because Gabriel says if you had so much food, how come you only ate one meal a day in the evening, but Paco says that was just because Harry Jack was so busy all day.

At night, after a hard day's work and a good meal, Harry Jack would tell Paco stories from his life. It was supposed to help Paco get to sleep, but the stories were too good for that. Harry Jack used to be a prospector in California and Mexico, looking for gold and silver. After that he ran a detective agency in Mexico City, but somebody tricked him and he had to run away. He opened a general store in Nueva Rositas but the authorities found him and took away all his money, so after some more prospecting and one lucky night in a Georgetown casino, he came here and started a new life. He told Paco he had been married five times, twice to the same girl, but all his wives were either dead now or turned out to be "two-timing whores only out for the god damned bucks."

Harry Jack always haggled with his customers, Paco says. Everything in the store had a price, but Harry Jack would always ask for more so that he could bargain. If it was an Indian he would sell for less, but if it was a rancher or a rich person the price would go up. He was the same with the traders who came to sell him things. He loved haggling, and sometimes he would argue over the price of a ten-cent bag of sugar just for the fun of it.

One day a rancher came to buy a clay pipe and Harry Jack told him it was an antique and would cost a hundred dollars in New York but he could have it for a hundred and ten as a special favour. The rancher told Harry Jack he was crazy, and that in any case the pipe already had a price ticket on it saying six dollars so what was he talking about? Harry Jack said the six dollars was just the tax, which he'd forgotten about, so that made a hundred and sixteen altogether. The rancher asked him when was the last time he ever paid any tax, and what he'd do if he just walked out of here, and Harry Jack said, "Well, amigo, if you do that I guess I don't sell the pipe, but no smokie for you-oo!" Paco always tells that story with Harry Jack's voice, singing the last little bit, and then laughs at the memory of Harry Jack.

HALF PAST

It was the madness of clocks that drove Harry Jack out of here and turned the store into a museum. Paco says it was a madness that crept up on you and at first it seemed like fun, but eventually the ticking of clocks changed Harry Jack, and he became just a little bit crazy. It all started when Harry Jack said to Paco one day, "Paco, amigo, what we need is a clock. That god damned cockerel's no good. We're always waking up late and missing out on trade. What we need is a clock to tell us what time it is and then we'll know when to get up and open the store."

They didn't open the store that day. Harry Jack rode straight off to the city. He came back the next day and banged a clock down on the counter for Paco to look at. It was the first clock he had ever seen. It had a case of polished mahogany. Harry Jack showed him how to wind it, and the little drawer in the back for the key. He said, "Paco, this clock is your responsibility. It's your job to wind it every night before you go to bed. You do your job with this clock and we'll never be late up again!" Then he laughed and went out in the back yard and shouted at the cockerel, "Are you listening, you old cockerel? We've got us a clock now. You're out of a job. You're going to be our next dinner!" Then he slapped his legs and laughed his big laugh. Paco laughed too.

Paco says every day after that Harry Jack would go out in the yard and yell at the cockerel and tell him he was their dinner for that day and how much he was going to enjoy cooking him now they had a clock. But every evening Harry Jack would swear about the cockerel and say how he was so old and tough he was going to make a pair of shoes out of him instead. He carried on like this every day. Every morning he shouted at it, walking right up to it and shouting about his special recipe for roast chicken, and every evening he cursed it for being too old and tough for cooking, saying how worn out his old boots were and how the cockerel's skin would be "just the god damned job" for the kind of leather he needed to make a new pair.

Harry Jack kept on like this for a whole month. Then one morning he said to Paco, "The trouble with this clock is it's too quiet. It tells the time all right, but what's the good of that if you're not awake to see it? The truth is, we're no better off now than we were before. We've got the clock to tell us the time but all it ever tells you is how god damned late you are for work." Then he told Paco about a special kind of clock he had seen in the city, specially made with big bells on the top to wake you up at the right time. *That* was the kind of clock they needed.

Paco didn't believe him at first. He told Harry Jack that it must be a trick because how would the clock know when you wanted to wake up? That made Harry Jack laugh his biggest laugh. He couldn't stop laughing and laughed so hard he tipped over his chair and broke it. Harry Jack just looked at the broken chair and laughed harder than ever. He said, "That's a good one that is, Paco. How will the clock know!" He kept saying over and over, "How will the clock know?" and roaring with laughter until he fell over the broken pieces of chair. Even then he didn't stop laughing. He just lay in the middle of the broken chair and laughed until he couldn't laugh any more.

That same day Harry Jack went back to the city and bought an alarm clock. Paco thought it was the most wonderful and clever thing in the world, the way it would wait until just the right time to ring the bell and wake you up. Harry Jack said that was nothing compared to some of the clocks they had in the city. They had big ones as tall as a man, and glass ones where you could see all the workings; they even had one with a little bird in it that came out every hour and sang to you. Paco laughed at this and told Harry Jack to stop telling silly stories. That made Harry Jack laugh too. He put his arms around Paco and said it was true, and he'd see soon enough because he was going to go back when he had enough money and buy one of the bird clocks.

That was how it started, and soon it became a regular thing. Every month or so Harry Jack would load up his horse and go off to the city. Sometimes he would be gone for two or three days, but every time he came back there was a new clock to look at, and one more job for Paco to do at bedtime.

For a long time the cuckoo clock was Paco's favourite, but one day Harry Jack brought home a wooden clock with a little house and garden under the dial, all painted in bright colours. When the clock chimed a little man and woman came out of the house and into the garden and kissed each other. They kissed once for each number of the hour, and then they walked backwards into the house again. Paco thought it was marvellous. Every time it chimed the hour he would run to look at the lovers in their garden, and try to find the magic of its working. Paco says he remembers the day Harry Jack brought this clock home especially, because that was the day he put his arms around Paco and asked him how would he like to have a little brother or sister to play with? Paco said he would like that more than anything.

Soon Harry Jack's shop was well known for its clocks. He had most of them in the shop and people would come to look at them. He got a lot more customers now because of the clocks. It was very noisy when the hour came round, but Harry Jack liked the noise and laughed when the clocks went off. These days Paco usually comes out of the museum just before the hour strikes, unless there are people in there. He says the noise is a little bit crazy, just like Harry Jack was.

But one day Harry Jack changed. He came back from the city with another new clock, but this one was broken, and he was in a bad temper. His eyes were red, but Paco couldn't tell if that was from crying or drinking. He had never seen Harry Jack cry, except from laughing.

After that day Harry Jack didn't laugh the same any more. For a few days he was very quiet. He would put his arms around Paco, but he would not say anything. At night the cooking had no laughter, and the stories at bedtime were not the same. The store was open in the day, but Harry Jack was like a wagon with a broken wheel, and he only charged the price on the ticket.

Harry Jack never went to the city again. He started drinking, and many nights he went out gambling in the town. He had always been a good gambler. Some nights he lost, but many times he won. He would come back happy then, and show his winnings to Paco, but still he did not laugh the same as before. Paco did not know what was wrong, but he felt sorry for Harry Jack.

They had more money now, from the gambling, and Harry Jack bought a little pony for Paco to learn to ride. Paco loved the pony, but not as much as he loved and missed the old ways of Harry Jack.

QUARTER TO

One night Harry Jack went out gambling and didn't come back until the next night. Paco was very worried until Gabriel told him there was a game in the mountains far away. Paco had heard of these games. They were played in the mountains where the Indians could join in. The Indians didn't have any money, but they had gold sometimes, or silver.

It was very late when Harry Jack came back, covered in dust from a long ride. Paco was so glad to see him, but Harry Jack didn't hug him, he went straight to a little box under his bed and pulled out some papers. He was in a hurry, and Paco says there was a strange look on his face like fear and happiness both together.

Harry Jack said he had found something in the mountains, something you couldn't even imagine. The game was still on and he needed to raise the stakes. Then he said he was playing against "a gang of god damned cheats," and it would take more than luck to win. He couldn't even stop to eat. He took Paco's pony and rode straight out.

Paco waited another three days. He talked to Gabriel, who didn't know anything about the game except that it was far away. Gabriel said not to worry, but just keep the store open and wind the clocks as usual. He said it was time Paco learned to cook anyway.

It was gone midnight when Harry Jack staggered into Paco's room. He needed help to carry something big and heavy into the store. Paco remembers hearing the wagon move off as they struggled with the clock of real time, putting it gently on top of a wooden crate in the back room, where it still is today.

When he turned up the lamp, Paco saw Harry Jack's coat was covered in a strange white dust that seemed to sparkle with hundreds of tiny stars like grains of crystal. The clock of real time was covered by a cape of Spanish leather. This also was dusty with the shining dust. But Harry Jack's face was grey with the dust of riding, and his eyes still had that strange look of being frightened and happy.

Then Harry Jack spoke the words that changed Paco into the museum keeper he has always been. He told him about the clock of real time, how it worked without winding, how to read it from seven in the morning on the first dial and four in the afternoon on the second dial. He told him how people would come to see the clock who should not be allowed to see it, and how to ask the pendulum question: what must we say to one who offers knowledge? He taught Paco how to understand the different answers. Paco says this was so clear he never had to write it down, and that it felt like the thing he had been trying all his little life to understand. Paco says it is a very simple thing to tell, but that some people can fool him with words which are well said, and when they do it is their own fault what happens to them.

Paco says Harry Jack explained everything very fast, then he had to go. He hugged Paco and told him he was a brave boy, and he knew he was leaving the clock of real time with exactly the right person. Paco started to cry, but Harry Jack said not to be afraid and to think about the clock and what time it showed: Harry Jack's time was nearly over, but there was one more thing to do, something he had been wanting to do for a long time. He had been afraid before, but now he was ready.

Harry Jack loaded up his horse, which Paco could see was already half dead, and went to say goodbye to Gabriel. It was dawn when he rode away on Paco's pony with the tired horse following behind. Paco cried and cried. He says Gabriel was crying too as they waved goodbye, but Gabriel says that is untrue. He says it was just very early in the morning and he wasn't feeling well. Paco says Gabriel is just an old liar whose life will never amount to anything. Gabriel says Paco should look at himself: taking care of a lot of clocks no-one wants to see, and living on army charity. He says Harry Jack came to this town with nothing but a pile of worthless foreign dollars, a toolbox and a broken down old horse, and that's exactly what he took with him when he left.

Paco and Gabriel like to argue. I only listen. But I like it too in a way. The riders don't pass this way much anymore, and I like to hear people talking as I sit in the street building up the colours on the flag.

OUTLAW HEART

My God, my God, why have I forsaken thee?

Given often to the fancy that God placed thoughts with him in answer to such prayers, Mark heard now an answer. It pounded through his mind to the rhythm of his walking; a walking so accelerated that it showed no care for the slender seven-year-old girl clattering along beside, slightly behind him, attached at the hand, in his frantic, stork-like march across the common towards the bridge where, God willing, deliverance awaited in the form of one last chance.

It is because, went the answer, *you have only ever in your entire life considered yourself. You and your miserable imaginings have conspired to cage Me in with bars of order and security. You have never embraced risk, which is My nature, nor courage, which is My smile, and so you have never given Me your allegiance. Instead, like the white ball on the carefully arranged pool table over which you bend so long and often, you have retreated on the instant of every break, fleeing the chaos you have engendered with such optimistic purpose the moment before.*

But this was just the latest in a series of answers. Mark had found himself asking the question many times these last few days. The question was haunting him, and God's reply was different each time. *It is because*, He told Mark yesterday, *you are trying to hurt Me, to make Me go out to find you or welcome you back.*

At other times the reply would be deeper for its brevity. Last night, just before sleep, Mark had heard *Because you want to* in an offhand, arms-folded tone of voice, and late this morning God had said in a doomy, emphatic, vaguely threatening tone, *I don't know.*

There was no need to walk so fast. He had to be in the old boathouse by eight o'clock, several minutes away, but Mark needed to keep himself in a brisk, positive state of mind. His resolve could easily crumble in front of Webster. Webster himself had taught him: if you're going to take the risk you have to see it through in every detail, no matter what. So when the plan had first arrived, like a malign foetus in the womb of his bitterness, Mark saw immediately its extreme possible consequences. And once he had decided to go all the way on one last chance or perish in the attempt, then immediately he knew he would need a gun.

That gun was in his jacket pocket now. He wasn't expecting to use it tonight; he had bought it for the getaway on Monday; but he thought a real outlaw would bring it along, just in case.

The girl held her free hand up to press her hearing aid back into place. Her elbow stuck out awkwardly, flapping like a clipped wing. Would she ever learn to relax? Not with a father who took her on missions like this. But that was all part of the plan.

Webster had never met Leila. He knew Mark had a daughter, but he didn't know how pretty she was, and he had probably forgotten that she was deaf. Nearly deaf. The hearing aid often emitted squealing feedback from its efforts to get audible volume for poor Leila. Well, today was Friday, and on Monday they would begin the trek back to Shropshire, to Margaret and reconciliation and a new hearing aid bought from some fat money at last.

And it was fitting that Leila should be involved, because it was dear Leila, the dearest, closest thing to his heart, who had pushed him over the edge in the first place. It was Leila who had prompted him to stay with Margaret just when he was about to leave. With Leila's arrival Mark had bowed to God's will and tried to be a good father. He tried hard, slowly surrendering bits of his freedom, time and money.

The loss of his job didn't make any real difference to his circumstances, but a year of unemployment left him frustrated and bored. With the discovery of Leila's deafness came grey ugly waves of depression. He started going out every day ostensibly looking for work, but the real reason was a combination of Margaret's moaning and his growing infatuation with the pool table. As his game improved he won a few small bets, then a few bigger ones, and eventually he was able to fund his activities without dipping into his dole money.

Throughout this time one factor made his life less than unbearable: the precocious beauty of his daughter. The girl was magical in her looks and personality. In the early years Mark would wear his daughter like a badge. People were forced to look at him with kind eyes because of the calm, silent, beguiling child beside him. Leila brought an expression of patient, benign puzzlement to all she encountered. Her pained, vulnerable, knowing eyes transformed everything they saw into something harmless and understandable. It was not the purity of her skin nor the radiance of her hair; her power stemmed from a diffidence straight out of Arthurian chivalry. She strolled through an alien urban chaos and rendered it sylvan. She was a walking benediction, a state of grace on legs.

And yet she would never relax. Mark discovered that her limbs, which seemed to glide through every landscape, were in fact in a permanent state of seizure. The storm of stiffness in her muscles would outlast the longest of his loving cuddles. Even when she was asleep she would lie stiffly, akimbo arms outside the covers, her frown betraying the sham tranquillity of her smooth eyelids and long lashes.

Halfway along the downward slope of the footbridge a small wrought-iron gate led through the stucco wall to a series of stone steps. Leila followed her father down to the ground and along a thin dirt track behind high sprawls of nettles and bindweed. The hum of the traffic was replaced here by the rustling of willow leaves and the muted slaps of the river. This was not noticed by the girl but her eyes were drawn to the willows and the tall shadowy boathouse hiding in their midst. The path led to the dark wooden wall of the boathouse and stopped abruptly at the ruins of a door.

Mark knew he was on university territory, but he also knew that the boathouse was abandoned and had been since his childhood.

The college had built its replacement forty yards upriver and had left the old one to follow its own slow process of decomposition. Curtained by the trees, it loomed darkly in the shadows. Its wooden plank walls were still intact, but years of neglect had left them dry, cracked, rotten. As Mark pushed open the door a shower of powdered wood hung like a ghost for a moment just inside the frame, partially illuminated by the pale light which leaked in through cracks and holes in the main doors facing the river.

Inside, the floor was hard-packed earth, surprisingly uneven. A few nettles could be seen at the edges where planks had rotted or broken away, but nothing grew behind that crumbling borderline.

Mark held Leila's hand and guided her behind the door to a tall steep stairway leading to an upper floor some twelve feet above the ground. The stairs had managed somehow to remain sturdy; each step brought forth a quiet creak that was almost a purr, as if the timber were secretly grateful to be used again.

The upper floor, however, was as dry and dusty as death. A solitary cobwebbed window looked out over the river, allowing a gloomy echo of light to creep apologetically into the middle of the room. Every floorboard rasped out a complaint as Leila crossed to the window and looked out at the fading evening. Her father spoke loudly a nervous warning.

"Careful, this floor might not hold. It's more like paper than wood."

The girl fiddled with her receiver. There was a faint crackle from her earphone.

"Uhh?"

"Watch the floor," Mark reiterated. "Look, it's disintegrating."

"You're heavier than me." Leila kept her eyes on her father. Her deafness gave her a breathy lisp which removed most of her consonants; Mark often had to search her eyes for the exact meaning in her voice. Her alert, serious face now made it clear that her reply had not been petulant but a sincere concern that he should consider his own safety. Tenderness quaked inside him for a moment, but he reminded himself of the need to be resolute tonight in front of Webster.

"Okay, now remember, this man we're meeting tonight is not a terribly *nice* man. He probably won't be kind to you. Just stay quiet and stay close to me."

Nevertheless tonight Leila would be his badge again. She would show Webster his sufferings and need of understanding. She would bring her brave puzzled expression to Webster's face and find a way to tap whatever paltry store of mercy lay within him. If anyone could do it, she could. And if it worked, and if the double-cross went as planned, then Webster might just decide okay, he deserved a break, let him go. After all ...

Mark's memory went back to those early successes gambling at pool, and the smoky clubroom where he had first met Whispers. He tried to remember Whispers' real name. He had been told it once. But everyone called him Whispers. He was a man who never spoke anything out loud, face to face. He didn't actually whisper his words, but everything was always somehow a secret, confidential; a tip here, some exclusive information there. Whispers never spoke to a group, always a word in your ear away from the others.

At first Mark tried to shrug off the attentions of this spindly, cloth-capped, gabardined figure, but for some reason Whispers had persisted with him and before long Mark was drinking at his table and meeting his cronies. There was never much talk, and what there was seemed deliberately coded. Mark gave up trying to understand it. But the name of Webster cropped up most nights, often dominating the sporadic bouts of conversation.

Whispers began giving Mark occasional tips on the horses. Mark was cautious at first, but he found that more often than not, Whispers was right; and when the info carried the magic prefix, "Webster says..." the horse *always* came in first, usually on good odds too. Eventually, and long before they met, Mark came to trust in Webster's name. Then one night, quietly casual, Whispers brought them together at the drinks table.

Webster's appearance was, Mark found, stunningly ordinary. Average height, medium build, unobtrusively dressed, nothing about him stood out, except perhaps a hint of coldness in the eyes; as if he was making a note of everything about you, from the cut of your clothes to the length of your fingernails.

Meeting Webster accelerated the pace of Mark's existence. His life quite literally changed from that moment. Other meetings followed, in a variety of pubs and clubs, and always with the same gang of half a dozen racetrack veterans: two tick-tack men, three ex-jockeys and an ageing stablehand.

Mark felt flattered by Webster's interest in him. Webster was a keen interviewer, willing to hear all Mark's opinions and troubles. When Margaret discovered Mark's betting habits and moved back to her parents' home in Shropshire, Webster was the first person Mark told. Leila's decision to stay with her school and established friends made things more difficult than ever. To help him out, Webster brought Mark in on his "little scheme."

Webster's tactics were simple and, characteristically, safe. On a given day, when a race was going to be won by an outsider, Webster handed out stake money to his team. Everyone chose a different betting shop. The winnings, never suspiciously massive, were collected and Webster gave his men half, minus the stake. His total was always substantial but no bookie ever got seriously hurt so no one made a fuss. With operations restricted to one every few weeks, Webster's system provided a pleasing, secure supplement to his other, reputedly less savoury earnings in London.

For several months Mark played his part in this system, then one morning Webster phoned him to arrange a special meeting; a *secret* meeting, he urged, with nobody else to know, not even Whispers. Three nights later Webster brought Mark to the old boathouse. There, by torchlight, he announced his new scheme, a special plan conceived strictly for the two of them, designed to put thirty thousand pounds in Mark's pocket and four times as much in his own.

"It's gonna require a bit of play-actin', Markie, but I *know* you can do it." In the wintry darkness of the boathouse Mark had not felt so sure, but he listened to the quiet confidence of Webster's jaunty tone as the plan was outlined.

"See, what you gotta *do*, my old son, is get yerself in with yer bookie, makin' good steady bets with *no system*. No system a-tall, yuh get me? And these bets, they *don't win*, not hardly any of 'em. Just the odd few now an' then come up trumps for ya. Don't worry, old son, I'll feed you the dosh when you need it. But all the *time*, like, it's all just guessin' an' hunchin'. You're always bettin' on a *feeling*, yuh get me?

"Now, what you gotta do is to get that old bookie to swaller your act, that's the thing. So he won't think nothin' of you stickin' fifty on a 'cumulator just when the fancy takes yer."

"Fifty *quid*?"

"Now don't worry, it won't take long, believe me, not if you choose the right bookie. I'll check it out for yer before we start. Only don't tell a soul, Markie, cos it's just you an' me on this one, all right?"

"Why not the others?"

"Oh, Markie, my dear old son, they ain't got the *brains* for it, know what I mean? They couldn't act their way out of a *brewery* now could they? Nah, it's only you what's got the brains for it. Matter of fact it was you what give me the idea in the first place. Now *lissen*.

"Come next summer there'll come a day, Markie, a little old day you'll put your fifty on a trio of big ones, and by Christ, Markie, they'll *all* come up! Your bookie's gonna fill his *socks* when that final 'orse comes in! Gotta be a big firm, Markie. We don't want no-one to go bust over it. But even so, that bookie of yours is gonna fill his trousers when that bastard comes up trumps. They'll be takin' Ex-Lax off the *market*! Now lissen!"

Mark kept it all to himself. He didn't tell Leila and he didn't tell Whispers, and the others weren't really his friends anyway. But there was something strange in this that didn't quite fit.

It was Webster's carefulness that finally gave him the key to the puzzle. He could not understand why a man who took such detailed precautions should entrust this operation to an unknown like Mark. Lying in bed one night, with Leila's tense protruding limbs conspiring to deny him sleep, Mark suddenly tumbled to the real extent of Webster's scheme. He was, of course, playing the same game with *all* of them. Mark, Whispers and the other six, all eight of them were operating the plan! And all secretly, under strict orders not to tell a soul.

And of course that put a whole new perspective on the thing. That explained why Webster was taking this risk for such a relatively small sum. Because it *wasn't* a small sum at all. Nothing like. Webster was going to be able to retire with grace from the whole grubby business of doping and fixing, bribing and bullying. And at ten grand apiece for the players, who was going to grumble?

That same night Mark decided that *he* would do the grumbling. After all, thirty thousand pounds was not really that much. Not enough to buy back his old life. It wouldn't buy new ears for the princess sleeping beside him. But four hundred grand was a different matter. With four hundred grand he could go back to Margaret and they could start again. They could hide themselves away somewhere, maybe in Wales, and buy a bit of land somewhere even Webster wouldn't know about. Because if Webster ever caught up with him …

Getting the gun proved surprisingly difficult. It was luck in the end: his bookie was getting rid of one and allowed Mark to buy it in advance of his gun club membership coming through. It was only a thirty-two, but even that seemed huge to Mark as he weighed it in his hand late one June night after putting Leila to bed. The dull heaviness of the metal frightened him. It was too honest. It made no attempt to disguise its function. And yet even Mark felt seduced by the glamour of the thing. The smell of it had a strange effect on his bowels and for a moment he felt sick. Wrapping it in a brown paper bag and hiding it away in a kitchen cupboard, a half-remembered verse of scripture came to him and emerged, altered, from his lips: "My God, my God, why have I forsaken thee?"

An ear-splitting crack scattered Mark's thoughts. For one deranged second he thought the gun had gone off in his pocket. Then he saw Webster's figure in the gloom at the top of the stairway. The floorboards had announced his arrival.

"Hello Webster," Mark gasped in an effort to regather his concentration and alert Leila who, behind him, might not have heard the noise.

"Hello Markie me old son." Through a series of shrieking footfalls as Webster approached, his voice carried a cold blade of suspicion. "What's the idea of bringin' the girl, Markie?"

"Oh, the babysitter couldn't make it tonight. Bit of a last minute job, I'm afraid."

Mark looked forward longingly to Sunday night when the babysitter would be paid off for the last time. He wouldn't be banking his winnings until they got to Shropshire. It would be fun crossing the country with Leila beside him and a snatched bag of money in his luggage. They would be outlaws on the run. Webster could never be anything so bold or brave as an outlaw; he was merely a criminal.

Now in the final fragments of available daylight the criminal stood face to face with the outlaw and was not the first to flinch. Mark turned and brought Leila forward.

"Leila, this is my friend, Webster."

Webster flicked his eyes at the girl for a moment. She smiled at him, serene and studious.

"What's with the microphone, Markie?"

"It's Leila's phonic ear. Hearing aid."

Webster's voice rose with curiosity and fear. "What's it do then? Tape it all up does it?"

"Oh no." Mark tried to chuckle. "No, it's like a radio."

"I don't like it, Markie. Turn it off, will yer? An' tell the girl to wait outside, there's a good boy. Gotta keep it secret, you know that."

Reluctantly, nervously, Mark obeyed. He adjusted the receiver on her ear and mimed to her as he spoke. "Here you are, darling, you go and wait outside. We'll only be a few minutes." Placing a hand on each of her taut shoulders, he was about to kiss her when Webster interrupted.

"Tell 'er to leave that thing here."

"What?"

Webster became impatient. "Come on, Markie, I got a lot to do! I ain't got all *night* you know!"

Mark placed the earpieces in his pocket. They clicked quietly against the gun, and he transferred them to the other side. He motioned Leila downstairs. "Won't be long," he said, though he knew she could not hear him. Leila's graceful steps crackled across the floor and down the stairs.

Webster pulled an envelope from his jacket and waved it at Mark. "This is it, my boy, this is the one. Are ya fit for it?" Mark did not reply. Webster looked doubtful, but he launched into the instructions in a firm, authoritative voice.

"Now *lissen*. There's three names in here, and three times, all right? You wanna get in early with that first one, old mate, coz the odds are bound to shorten on that before the off. The third one's the real bobby dazzler, though. That'll *really* put the cat amongst the bags, don't you worry. They're all on at the same course. You'll find *that* in the paper.

"Now play it straight, Markie, play it normal. Just be your normal self, that's the first thing. The other thing is, go in as normal on the Mondee, all right? Collect your winnings. They'll want to make a fuss but you tell 'em, no pictures. You should 'ave your bookie on *your* side if you've played it right. Whatever they say, you don't want *no* publicity. Now, don't take any notice of *me*. Don't show you know me. Jus' take the dosh round to the bank and wait for me there. I'll follow you out but you don't even *look* at me, is that clear? Are you getting' this straight, Markie?"

Webster's last question had a strained, suspicious tone. He leaned into Mark's face, searching his eyes. Mark had not been listening at first. He had been angrily reviewing Webster's treatment of Leila: the hurtful way he had first ignored, then dismissed her; his complete failure to show sympathy or interest. Mark had felt it like a slap in the face. Rage and fear boiled up, threatening his composure. But he had heard the last bit, the bit about Webster being with him for the pay-off, and that had dropped like a depth-charge into his submerged strategy.

"You mean ..."

"Wot, Markie? What's the matter?"

"Nothing, but ..." His mind flailed for a sensible response that might put Webster off. A secret disappearance was one thing, that would be easy. But grabbing the whole bagful of loot and running with Webster right behind him was a risk he found too tricky to countenance. "There's no need, though ..."

"No need for what, Markie?"

Mark found himself staring full into the shadowed eyes a few inches from his own. Had he given himself away? It was Webster's instinct to suspect and mistrust. Had he already said too much? Panic produced a lame inspiration.

"No need ... to actually go to the bank, is there? Can't we just..."

"Oh I see! No, I always like to handle big money in a bank, my old son. Play it safe, that's my catch-word." Webster waved the precious envelope in Mark's face. He sounded relaxed, almost relieved, but his eyes remained on Mark's. In the relative calm of the moment, Mark realized there was a simple way of avoiding Webster's manoeuvre. It was an idea Leila herself might have come up with, from the clever little pig in the story she used to love: turn up an hour early, enjoy the fair, and get away before the wolf has even arrived at the meeting place.

"What time?"

"Time, Markie?"

"What time should I turn up on Monday?"

"Oh, your usual time, me old son." Webster paused, dropping his head slightly so that he looked up at Mark. Then, in a casual tone he continued, "Usual time. Play it normal. I'll be there when they open."

Whatever it was that Mark's face did – a slight widening of the eyes, perhaps, or a brief flinch on one side – it was enough to reach across five inches of gloom in the boathouse to the waiting eyes of the criminal. Webster stepped back a pace, puncturing the silence with a grinding wooden clack.

"Jesus! Bastard! You total bleedin' bastard!"

"What?" Mark gasped, frightened by Webster's behaviour.

"The money, Mark," Webster sneered. "The bloody money!"

"What money?"

Webster paused, apparently reflecting. "*Your* money, you toe-rag bastard! I don't like the *colour* of it, Markie. It's *yellow*. Bleedin' *yellow* money. Like the streak down your back! You were gonna fleece me, weren't ya! After all I've done for you! You were gonna take me to the fleecers!"

Mark took a step toward him. "You've got it wrong, Webster. What are you talking about? What did I do?" The creak of Mark's advancing footstep was answered by two of Webster's in retreat. In the near darkness Mark saw the white envelope containing his entire future disappear into the void of Webster's jacket.

"Don't come near me, you creepin' git! You don't know the half of what you've done, you bastard! This is bigger than you think. Well it's all off for you, mate. You're out of it, and your pay-off is one big nothing!"

The pocketing of the envelope gave Mark his signal. He reached into his own pocket and his hand was filled with cool metal. He lifted it out slowly and pushed it at the shadowy form in front of him. Now pops and cracks punctuated the talk as the two men edged in parallel towards the stairs.

"See this, Webster? It's loaded. Don't move. Give me the envelope."

Webster continued his slow, crackling withdrawal. "You can't afford it, mate. Believe me, what you wanna do is get out of here. Tell you what, I'll give you a break." He stepped forward, splitting the air with noise, and gestured at the stairway. "There you are, old son. I'll wait five minutes, then we'll never see you again. You can't say fairer than that, now can yer?"

The raucous wood stopped its noise. The window's pale light was away from them here, by the steps. Webster's white shirt was visible; everything else was vague dark brown and grey. Mark's world centred now on the envelope hidden near the whiteness. That envelope contained his one last chance. It could open out a bright Monday afternoon on the road to the west: Shropshire, Margaret, an outlaw ride across the country. He found himself aching for the right words to come. It was like a prayer. Dear God, give me an outlaw heart; give me an outlaw's words.

"I mean it, Webster. It's too late to turn back now. You're a criminal. You don't understand."

For the first time Webster seemed to believe in the gun. His voice had a tone Mark had not heard before.

" Mark! Markie boy! Let's just ferget it, all right? Tell you what, *I'll* go. I'll just run along now and you keep mum. Keep mum and I'll see you're all right."

Mark stirred himself for the final desperation, the squeezing of the trigger to take him out of this darkness. What would a criminal do? Just blast him in the gut, probably. But an outlaw needs a heart. He wasn't a crook; he couldn't be a killer. So Mark aimed down at Webster's leg. Just a shot to wing him, to bring him down and take that precious envelope.

Webster stepped back a fraction. The floorboard creaked slowly. Mark saw the movement. It was now or too late forever. Peering into the dark, he pulled crisply on the trigger. The gun exploded the moment with a sound that was too thin and piercing to be a roar. Mark felt a pain in his ears and a sudden ache in his wrist. The wooden walls seemed to shudder as if shaking off a coat of dust. A wisp of powdered wood puffed into the air by Webster's feet, unnoticed in the darkness, as the bullet clipped through the floor.

Webster's response was immediate.

"Okay, Markie! Here you are. Here's the envelope. It's yours." His words sounded distant, muffled by a humming in the ears. "It's all yours, Markie, okay? You take it an' my *blessin'* on yer." He reached into his pocket. "You take the money on Mondee too. It's yours to keep, okay? Buy the little girl a noo dress." He forced a laugh. "Buy 'er a noo buggin' device, ay? He held out the envelope. Mark grabbed it and Webster vanished down the stairs.

Leila hardly heard the gunshot. She had been sitting on the lower steps where she had dawdled, waiting for her father, and the bullet had sped through the powdery wood straight into her heart, where it lodged like a tiny lump of fire. She was still sitting there as Webster clattered past her, flung back the door and disappeared into the cool blue of the late evening shadows.

Mark stared into the blackness. He felt dazed and tired. His shirt was sticky with sweat. One hand gripped his prize, his future, almost weightless; the other held the two pounds of metal that had made possible his deliverance. The fear he had held back in the struggle with Webster suddenly roared through him and he shook, breathing out heavily, still staring at the dark. He felt the cold of the night for the first time and shivered out of his trance. The pain in his wrist nagged him. He put the gun in his pocket but held on to the envelope as he turned toward the stairs.

The floorboards cracked out their dry protest each time he shifted his weight and groped in the dusty darkness for the handrail. Then, shuffling across to the opening, he skipped down the steps to the ground, where he dropped his burden and gathered up his beautiful daughter to hold her, perfectly relaxed now at last, in his arms.

GRIEVOUS

"Young Harry, he were a lad."

The old man's off on one of his stories again. He's a killer for stories, the old man. Sunday lunch is over, a recollection grabs him, out comes a story. Out of his mouth, out of his gleaming eyes. It's the gleam that gives the warning. Seconds later there'll be a chuckle from his thin, bony chest, and that's when Sue and Maggie groan and head for the back door fast. They never want the stories, Sue and Maggie. Billy and I usually stay, though. We used to stay out of courtesy, Billy and me; and I still don't know about Billy. Maybe even now Billy only sticks around because he feels sorry for the old man, worries he might be upset if we walk out in the middle of a story. I was the same for ages. But as the old man got older and more frail, and somehow wilder in his greyness and frailty, I found myself enjoying his stories more. It wasn't just pity, it was as if the stories became more important, more exciting, for the old man and for me.

To look at he's just another old man. He sits in his armchair in baggy, braced trousers of thick, coarse cotton. In the 'V' of his shirt you can see India burnt in red like the map, but the Indian Ocean is weak white milk, not blue. That's a farmer's neck. It doesn't fade in winter. He'll die with India under his chin.

I'm still young enough to get excited about coming down the farm. It's different for the others. Billy's a lot older than me, and so is Maggie. Sue's nearer my age but she's outgrown the farmyard thing. She's in a hurry to follow Maggie into town and flats and boyfriends. But I still like it when we visit. Every summer I stay a week down here. Sue used to come too but she has a week with Maggie now instead.

It's only through staying here that I've started to really like the old man. He's gruff, and he doesn't like having kids under his feet.

But watching him and Uncle Jack on the farm made me realise how hard it is on a small farm. The old man calls it God, Uncle Jack calls it the seasons, but whatever you call it, that's what they stake their lives on every year. I used to think I'd like to be a farmer myself, but now I'm looking around for something that'll kill me a bit slower. It's a twenty-five hour day and the odds are six-to-four against, here in Suffolk. That's what Uncle Jack says anyway. It's his farm now, of course.

The old man still works. Uncle Jack can't stop him. Uncle Jack never married. He looks after the old man, cooks for him. Eileen does their washing in Foxton. Eileen's about two hundred years old. She's got a two-room cottage with an outside Elsan loo, and a shining new Hotpoint automatic in the scullery. Uncle Jack bought it for her a couple of years ago, after Grandma died. It was the old man's idea. Trust Maggie to find proof of a scandal in that.

It's through Sue and Maggie that we call him the old man. We always used to call him Grandad, like any other family. But when Maggie reached independence and fashions she really kicked out against anyone born more than a couple of minutes before her. It was Maggie who started calling him the old man, and Sue picked it up straight away because she's always lived off Maggie's surplus stock. They said it with disgust at first but somehow it stuck, and eventually we all picked it up, even Mum. Of course we always call him Grandad to his face, but whenever we talk *about* him he's the old man. What's in a name?

Funnily enough, that's what the old man's on about just now. He's telling us about a boy called Harry; about his nicknames.

"His name warn't Harry, you know. No, it were George, his real name. George Bernard Harrison. But we called him Harry for short; from when he was a boy, ten or eleven. We always knew 'im as Harry but his friends... when he grew up and moved into town he picked up with some other young people like they do, and they used to call him Beetle. *Beatle*, you know, 'cause of one of them was called that same name, George Harrison, you see, in the *Beatles*! But then later, when he joined the army, he come back once with one of his army pals, and *he* used to call him Grievous! He told me everyone in the army called him Grievous on account of his initials, you see. G B H, grievous bodily harm.

"He warn't too happy in the army, I don't think. Mind you, he'd never show it. He were always smiling, was Harry. Always up to some lark or other. Every five minutes nearly he'd be off on some new idea. 'Wish me luck,' he always used to say. 'Wish me luck,' and off he'd go, cheerful as I dunno what. Yes, it'd take a lot to make Harry sore.

"He got sore over them white lions, though. Yes, bless me, oh."

He's laughing now, remembering it. His face is all creased up; his eyes, all tiny, shining out.

"See, he used to come down, as a boy, and help us out at weekends. I'd give him a trailer to load with straw, or later on he did a bit of tractorin' and I'd give 'im a bit of pocket money for it, see. We had 'im over them white lions, though. Let's see, he must've been about thirteen or fourteen then, and he come down on the Saturday to help me tile the roof of that shed out front. Well, after we'd been going half an hour, and it was hot, I said I didn't expect to see you this morning, Harry, on account of them white lions. 'What white lions?' he says, quick as a flash, 'cause he were always out for a lark, you know, was Harry.

"I says, 'Why, the white lions up at the village, of course, up at the station.' He looked a bit confused and shrugged his shoulders at that. 'I don't know about no lions in the village,' he says. I says, 'Well *surely* you've heard about the washing of the white lions, Harry? It happens every year. Every year they bring 'em down on the train, get them out at Foxton and scrub them down with brooms and water. This day every year at eleven o'clock.'

"Well, that stopped him working, you can bet. He arst me no end of questions about them lions, where they washt 'em and why they brung 'em down here. I carried on just casual like, just answering him matter-of-fact like. I told him it were all connected with the Foxton water, how it were good for their colour. 'Course, I told 'im all about how *rare* they was an' all, them being *white* lions an' everything. Pretty soon he's got a look on his face, sheer agony, on account of him having to stay here an' work while there's such a show on up at the village. He carried on workin', you know, but you could see his heart warn't in it.

"Just as it's comin' towards eleven, old Harry starts gettin' all thoughtful and sorrowful looking, and he says, 'I believe I'll go up at coffee time and just have a look at those old lions.' I says, 'Well you'd better git goin' quick, it's nearly eleven now.'"

From where I'm standing I can see through the kitchen window to the yard outside. Mum's in the far corner, sitting on a trestle, sunning herself. Uncle Jack's just finshed the washing up, and he's gone out to join her. Sue and Maggie are standing in the yard together, kicking the grass and laughing, at the old man's expense probably. I look down at the old man in his armchair, rattling off his memory with more confidence than he ought to have, really. What a funny old man he is.

"Soon as Mum calls out for coffee, he's down off that roof and into the kitchen. I don't know what Mum said to 'im, but he's come out the kitchen a lot slower than he went in. When I come in for coffee old Harry says, 'You nearly had me with that one, Mr Mason. I almost swallered it whole.' I says, 'What do you mean? It's true as I'm standin' here!' An' *that* confused 'im too, 'cause I'll generally own up if I'm caught out on a whopper, you know, an' he knows that all right. Then Mum starts up tellin' me not to lead 'im on so. Your grandma always did have trouble seein' the funny side."

Grandma's dead now. She died three years ago this August. They'd been married forty years and argued thirty-nine of them.

They seemed to thrive on it. The old man makes a virtue out of not showing his feelings. When Grandma died he went to stay with his brother in Somerset and didn't even go to the funeral. He came back two weeks later, when everything was settled, and just carried on without her. We felt a bit outraged by it, but Bernard, his brother, came down last summer and he told us in his usual quiet, confidential way that the old man had, "You know, cried a lot, old boy. Yes, cried quite a lot, oh yes." If God himself accused the old man of that I think he'd deny it.

"So while we're having coffee, I says to him, 'Well I shouldn't *want* you to go anyway, Harry. We need you here today on that roof.' That done it. He was off out that door and on 'is bike, you'da thought his britches was on fire. 'Wish me luck,' he says to Mum, and off out the door 'e goes."

Look at him. He can hardly get it out for laughing.

"'I'll wish you bloody luck!' she says. 'You come back here, young Harry!' She was sore. 'You damned old liar!' she says to me, 'You damned old bloody liar!' She was *livid*. She calls out to 'im, 'There's no more white lions up at Foxton than I'm a gorilla! Come back here and don't you be so stupid as to believe a word that damned old coot tells you.' Old Harry turns round his bike and comes sailing back round the yard. Course, I was roarin' by then."

There are tears all over the old man's face now. It's nearly three years since Grandma died.

"He comes back up the porch and he sees me laughin'. I was roarin' fit to bust, I was straight."

As he leans forward to laugh there seems to be a partial collapse of his body, but he slaps his knee and hoots his hot amusement even louder.

"'I'll get you back fer this one!' he says. 'Make a fool of me!' He slammed his bike down and shot back up the roof. He took it well, you know, oh, but he was sore."

The riot quelled, he slowly subsides. His head goes back on the cushion, his hands slide up his thighs to rest. He'll be asleep in a few minutes. Billy and me smile at each other. The story wasn't as funny as the old man's laughing face, but he won't know that. We laughed at his story, that's what counts to him, for us.

"Yeah, old Harry, he were a good'n. Good worker, oh yes. Never any trouble. Ain't seen 'im in years. Last time I saw him was that day he come back from the army with his friend. Two-day pass, they had; just time to say hello, he said. Stayed a couple of hours and off they went. Yeah, Grievous, they called 'im. But he warn't so happy, I don't think. Seemed *tired*, you know, and a bit anxious. Kept lookin' out the window all the time. Same old Harry, though, always chirpy. 'Wish me luck,' he always used to say; off he'd go.

"Funny enough, some more of his army pals come lookin' for 'im next day. Came by in a jeep. Arst me if I'd seen 'im. I told 'em he'd be back at camp by now with only a two-day pass. It was a puzzle at first cuz they called him George, but they called him Grievous too, so they knew him all right.

Sunday afternoon stillness is creeping over the farm. The old man surprises us both by springing up and stepping to the kitchen for more tea. It'll be cold by now but he'll drink it anyway. Billy and I walk through to the kitchen and stand around, ready to edge for the door once the old man's settled again. I expect we'll go for a walk with Mum and the others.

The old man empties his dregs in the sink, then goes to the table for his refill. Harry's still on his mind.

"Ain't seen 'im that day to this. Him and his mate. Same old Harry. 'Wish me luck.' He said it just the same when he went: 'Wish me luck.'"

His cup isn't quite set in its saucer. I hover in attendance as he rattles through to the sitting room and lowers himself slowly into his chair. The rattling stops. Staring ahead and stirring his tea, lost in his memory, he doesn't know I'm here. I'm just tiptoeing back to the kitchen when I hear him say, almost under his breath, "Good luck, Harry."

The others have gone on ahead. They're halfway to the forty-acre field as I step into the sunshine. Billy's a lot older than me, and I'm wondering now exactly what he's thinking. Did he hear what I heard just now? If so, we've both got a new angle on the old man. If not, am I still too young to think of these things, or should he be proud of me for not asking awkward questions about those 'pals' in the jeep?

In the forty acres the corn is tall, but still a little green. Good luck, Harry.

IN PRAISE OF NAHUM TATE

It's a long time since the girl stepped out of the garden. It was deliberate, and she got what she deserved: a hard time. That's what people say.

Who knows what triggered her departure? Not I. Maybe she just wanted to kick up some dust. Perhaps she had been in that garden too long and didn't appreciate it the way you or I would. Or maybe she didn't like some of the weeds that were growing there. Anyway, we're stuck with it now.

She went to stay in Europe for a while. By the time she got back she found the garden had gone completely to hell.

There are no fairytale endings. She didn't last long in that changéd place. Pale flower, she was caught in the gears of ambition and revenge, and her father did that one great sad thing no parent ever expects or wants to do: he saw her out.

Oh lord, there are no fairytale endings. But there was a man who tried to fix one up. Naturally he didn't fool anyone clever, and pretty soon it all started to look like a naïve, ignorant joke. Both the story and its telling became grotesque. With the passing of time the structure crusted with absurdity and fell derelict. You won't find anyone willing to tell the story that way now.

The fixer got it wrong, they say. His reputation collapsed, twisting into something very like his story. Everyone laughs at him now but that man, he is some kind of a friend of mine.

Now the winds are howling across the top of those cliffs. Solitary figures move on the plain, wrapped in folded cloth, casting shadows, frightened-looking and sad. One might hold a child, a boy, by the hand as if showing him a great wonder. The light comes from near the horizon.

FISHER OF MEN

"The Disciples became fishers of men," said the preacher, often.

But the fishermen of the town respected him not. "What does *he* know about fishing?" they sneered. "He never risked his life just to bring home a living for his family."

They knew about risk: the heaving, tipping heights of the sea were ever hungry for fresh-caught human.

They did not know his secret. As a young crewman he had snatched two lukewarm bodies from the ocean's tilting maw in the oily stench of a crippled, listing trawler. A third, whose hand he not quite grasped, plunged deep into a dark green swell, never to rise again.

Hailed as a hero, he found shelter with the church, called like a disciple from the shores of Galilee. He moved to a different coast and settled into a preacher's life, a fisher of men.

It never stopped hurting, the polished memory of a doomed, straining hand with its face of empty surprise. So the preacher spent every sermon reaching for that one lost soul. Arms wide, he would stretch out his hands in supplication, like a man who fishes with rod and line measuring out the one that got away.

You might encounter him yet if you are ever down that way, for he lives there still, preaching the gospel message: that through faith a man can be saved. You will perhaps know him by his fervent prayers for those in peril on the sea.

from CAPTIVE SILLY WOMEN

a novel

MARY

You won't explain me. I'll tell you before I even start several things that are true, and they'll *certainly* stop you explaining *me*.

For a start, I hate him. I absolutely hate him and have done for years. I was always frightened of him too. Right from the start.

And I respected him. He was the father of the children, he owned the house and ran the farm. All those things I respected him for. And I knew they gave him power so I feared him too. And that's why you'll never make sense of this, because all those things are different and they all happened at the same time, and at different times too. Sometimes *I* was different and sometimes *he* was.

Because we all change all the time. It's like we're different people every day. I'm different every day, but I'm still the same person too; there you are, explain that.

DON

Bellamy will tell you that this entire adventure came out of the blue. He'll believe it too. That's because one day I turned up at his house and told him what I was going to do and how he was going to help me do it. That was the first he knew about it.

But I'd been digging around for ages – phone calls, visits, spying, asking people in the pub, in the village, everything – building up the dossier on Mary, and especially that man.

That man, he hasn't got a friend in the world. He's a laughing stock and doesn't know it, because he's just so powerful that every time he calls in at the village store two and a half thousand acres of land trail in with him like the black, bloodstained wings of some poisonous bird of prey, and what they do, those wings, is smother honesty and proper relations, so that the old woman who works in the shop, who is actually very *nice* and only wants to pass the time of day with you, starts scuttling around like a rat in a trap saying yes sir no sir three bags full sir because there isn't just land on those wings, there's fields and trees and water, and *rights* to that water, and buildings and homes and jobs and families; there's futures and livelihoods on those wings and he not only *can* shake them off or swallow them up, he *will* if he gets crossed or if it just happens to suit him, and he *has* in the past and she *knows* that. She knows it better than most as a matter of fact, because the people he's done it to in the past used to go into that shop but they don't any more because they've gone and their money's gone with them. Or rather it *hasn't* gone with them, *he's* got it.

So for Bellamy it was all a bit of a shock when I turned up and said what are you doing Monday week because whatever it is you'd better cancel it, we're going to rescue Mary.

MARY

If I hadn't taken this job I would never have understood time. People think that everything you do is a decision. They look at you and say Oh, so that's what she did in the end, she went to work for that man, as if I'd had a whole row of choices and picked the best one. They think I could have chosen anything, and that all the choices were what I'd like, and if I chose nannying for *him* then that's what I wanted more than anything else from that whole range of things I could just as easily have done.

In fact I took the job because it came up and I didn't know what I wanted and I might as well do that until I *do* know what I want to do. But even that's not all of it. I took the job to see what would happen if I took it. I didn't have a plan. I didn't have a choice either. It didn't have anything to do with *me*. I arrived at being seventeen and the job came up, and I just happened to take it.

What could I do? I was seventeen, didn't have any education, there was nothing in the future.

I didn't have any feelings of loving children or anything like that. I could have been a packer. I could have been *anything*, except that there was nothing for me to be. Then I went for the interview and a man said I could be the nanny if I wanted to. I *didn't* want to. I just said All right I'll be a nanny. There's no choice in that.

I know I told lies at the interview. I said I loved children. I probably said I wanted to work with children. It doesn't matter what I said, it was all lies. But that's what everybody does. If you don't do that you don't get the job. You don't even get that, something you don't want.

You don't ring someone up and say I don't want the job you've advertised and then they say Okay you can have it. So what can you do? If you don't tell lies and pretend to be what they want, then you won't even have the choice of something you don't want. The only actual *choice* you have is whether to ring up in the first place. Once you've done that you're wasting your time if you don't put on an act of being what they want you to be.

But that's *my* business, all that lying. If I do the job okay, it doesn't matter if I'm Hitler or Mother Teresa. As long as I do the job, that's the only thing that matters, to them at least.

So I took the job and went to work for him and Lena. I moved in with them and that's what my life became. But don't tell me that's what I *chose* to do. It just happened.

I could have left any time. I thought I would. But that's just something that *didn't* happen. If I made any kind of decision you could say I decided to look after Toby and Dominic until it was time for me to do something else, but quite simply that time never came.

I think we change all the time. Don told me once about the molecules in your body, how they get replaced completely every so many years. So in that sense we really *are* different people. I've been lots of different people.

Living on the farm, seeing the seasons, it's taught me about time. Time used to drag by when I was at school. Now it rushes. You can't put into words what you think when you say, Marshall will be *ten* this year. I remember cuddling him on the bed and saying, "You are six weeks old and I am *twenty-one years!*" Now he seems older than me. I have seen the world turning by all this time, and now I can go along with it, but he is still anxious to hold on, to change and control things, as if these days are the only time he'll ever have. Even that is a change, because until a year or two ago, I used to tell him, "You'll see, all this straining and crying and effort is not necessary; you'll get where you're going when you get there, all you need to do is be ready, prepare yourself. But now I know he'll have to go on trying, bursting his guts over every tiny thing, because that's the only way he'll ever come to realise that trying is no good, that you can't control things, how many arms and legs have you got anyway, that you reckon you can put everything where you want it and hold it there, the people, the weather, the money, the buildings and vehicles, yes, even the time where you want them and in the right quantities *and* yourself too, just right and turning the corner just when you need to and arriving at that perfect arrangement which, even if you ever *did* manage to arrange for yourself, would immediately start changing and breaking up before your very eyes, before you would even have time to hold it and say it's mine?

So now I know it rushes, and I just say That's all right, you're in more of a hurry than I am, so go on along because I'll be here next spring and I've got some apples in the kitchen right now that need stewing, so if you don't mind I'll just get on with that; unless I'm *not* here next spring, in which case it won't matter anyway.

BELLAMY

I said, "Mary who?" I mean, that was my honest first reaction when he said it. Mary who? We've got this dude, this old friend of ours, who we haven't seen for something like *two years*, who finally turns up somewhere over in *Mexico*, for God's sake, and he suddenly comes bouncing into town, rolling in dough. He's, like, *wearing* more money than I see in a month, and that's just casual. So we see him a few times and we go out, you know, have a few beers and that. And everything's fine. I mean it's good to *see* him, don't get me wrong or anything. Him and me, we've been close for *ages*, years and years. And then one day here he comes, bopping all around my living room, snapping his fingers and talking twenty-to-the-dozen, and he suddenly turns around and says Cancel *every*thing, man, we're going out next week and rescue this chick. We're going to ride out to some farm in the middle of nowhere. You know, *Mission Impossible*. And we're going to go storming in and get this girl out, this chick, who he hasn't even *seen* for twelve years, and who ditched him in the first place, let's get *that* straight, and come back trailing clouds of glory. I mean, you've got to admit. You know, I'm just a simple man. Some things, I don't know, some ideas I just find take a bit of getting used to. I mean, I don't know what he expected.

I said, "Wait a minute, let me get this straight. There's a girl you haven't seen for twelve years. That's a hundred-and-forty-four calendar months. She gave you the elbow exactly one gross of menstrual cycles ago, and you've neither seen nor heard of her since, and she's been sitting around on her backside twiddling her thumbs in a Suffolk farmhouse all this time waiting for you to ride up and bring her back to civilisation? I'm sorry man, did I miss anything out? Is that what you're telling me here?"

He said, "That's it."

I said, "Well why wait till Monday? I've got half an hour before the football starts on the telly, let's go out and do it *now*, we can pick up Lord Lucan on the way back, no sense wasting petrol."

FOWLER

You have to keep your eyes open around here, and that's what I'm good at. I keep a close eye on everything that goes on, here on the farm and up at the village. You'd be surprised.

Mind, there's one or two things you *don't* see, and *that* tells you a lot too. I can't make it *all* out. I can't see how she and the old feller get along hardly a-tall. That's a damned strange arrangement they've got going on there and no mistake. So it's interesting what you don't see, as well as what you do.

There's *one* thing you won't see, and that's Lena's grave. You ask the old man, you even ask his *kids*, they'll tell you she died. I'm not saying *any*thing. I'm just saying, Where's the grave? Weren't no funeral. There ain't no headstone neither, up at church. I don't ask. I don't pry. He says she was buried in France, on holiday. Fine by me. I just wonder what happened to the Mercedes sports that picked her up to take her there. Fanciest taxi *I* ever saw. And what about the brown leather coat that was driving it? What happened to him? Same driver, same taxi what used to pick her up at the bus stop every Friday. Funny how he only got up the courage to go down the actual farmhouse on that one time he picked her up for the holiday. Must've been all that luggage she was bringing with her. Ideal for luggage, a Mercedes sports. Took her all of two seconds to slide the cash-box between her legs and under the seat.

I just keep an eye, though. I don't draw no conclusions. What's it to me if the old man spent that whole evening in the Swan sinking a bottle of brandy and playing pool with himself like he wanted to smash the balls to pieces with his stick? He made it clear he didn't want no chat with *me*. Me nor anyone. I went home early and sniffed round Bloody Mary. Nothing available there, of course. Never has been, never will be. She wasn't putting out and she wasn't telling, neither. I don't know how much she knew. You never *can* get anything out of her. *Talk*, I mean, not the other. Ha, she gives them away in roughly equal amounts, I'd say. God, that *would* be the day if she ever put out for *me*. The day I get a bit of tit off her, they'll be building igloos in Hell, I reckon. No, but she's a *dark* cow too. Never lets *anything* out. She wouldn't tell you your *trousers* was on fire unless the smoke was spoiling her washing.

I said goodnight to her about half nine, but I kept an eye out once I was in bed. There weren't but two lights blazing when he drove up about midnight: the outside light and her bedroom. That was the first time I'd ever seen *her* light on so late, but I've seen it lotsa times since. I don't say it *means* anything, I just take an interest in stuff. And I ain't saying I got any idea about what *else* happened that night neither. I don't reckon the rest of the world stays awake very often wondering much about Suffolk. All I do is keep an eye. I reckon probably it doesn't mean *anything* that he switched off the outside light about as soon as he got in, and I reckon it probably don't mean much more that there weren't any other lights switched on or off for the whole of the rest of that night.

Let's face it, I'm only a *young* man. I can't see much in the night time without there being a light on. All I saw was a shadow or two when it passed across the light. But he'd been living there fifty-three years by the time old Lena went. I reckon a man of fifty-three can see well enough in the dark to find his own room and get undressed and put himself to bed without needing a light on to do it with. Anyway, probably by that time he was so blind drunk a light wouldn't make any difference.

DON

Bellamy raised all sorts of objections. He listened very seriously to the idea.

His big brown eyes seemed to turn white when I first suggested it. He was sitting on the sofa and I was standing in the middle of the room. I can see him now. When I had finished he sprang up and started moving jerkily around the room, arms flailing about, fingers splayed. He *was* funny. His voice went up several tones and he started trying to tell me how loopy the whole scheme was. With his dark skin and the rolling whites of his eyes, the akimbo arms and wailing voice, I half expected him to start talking like Nigger Jim: "How's you gwine doo dat, Marse Don? Wit de Ess Ay Ess or sometin'?" But of course he still had that quick, rolling voice, very dark and serious sounding even when he was hysterical, which he was *now* in a way. He tried to explain to me, very gently of course and in the tones of a loyal friend, that I was basically a raving loony.

"Don, maybe you don't quite realise, man, but life *goes on*, even when you're away! Just because you haven't *seen* this girl for so long, that doesn't mean she's still *back* there in 1975, sweet sixteen and never bin kissed! Take a look at yourself. Are you the same as you were then? Am *I*? Look, I don't know if you spent a bit too long in the Mexican sun or *what*, but you can't expect her to just be waiting for you to come back and pick it all up again. Life isn't *like* that. You haven't seen her for *twelve years*. She's prob'ly married with kids and everything."

"No, she's still down there."

"How do you know?"

"I asked in the village."

"Even so, she already *gave* you the push once; how the hell do you think you're going to walk back into her life and start all over again? You're *both* different people now. You'd never make it fit."

"No, you're missing the whole *point*."

"Don, there *is* no point. I mean, you haven't even contacted her! Why don't you just get on the phone now and have a talk with her or something, and find out how she feels about you? Maybe she…"

"Because that's exactly the kind of dull, boring, sensible way of doing things that takes all the *spark* out of life, that's why. I've finished with all that. This whole damn country is full of good sense and the proper way of doing things. There's no *risk* anymore. There's no *romance*! I want her to see and hear me for the first time in twelve years, walking through that door to take her out of there. That's why I went to Mexico in the first place, to get away from all that drivel."

"Yeah, exactly. *You're* the one who's been away, not her. You're the one who's been to university, who's done teacher training, who's taught in Manchester and Macclesfield and then, God help us, friggin' *Mexico*! You're the one who's changed, Don, can't you see that? She's still down there in the heart of boring old England. She's going to take one look at you and your fantastic, romantic rescue mission and she's going to tell you to sling your hook, buster, and I for one won't blame her when she does! I mean..... Look, why did she drop you in the first place?"

That was simple. "I don't know, Bellamy. That's the honest truth now, I just don't know. But look, Bell, you're still not getting the idea of it. You're still not getting the point."

And then I told him. I gave him the full works. It just welled up inside me and I spoke it, like an apostle in the grip of the Spirit. It was one of the most powerful moments of my life. In Bobby Bellamy's living room on a quiet, sunlit Sunday afternoon, with just the occasional sound of children in the street and birds in the back garden, I just poured out all the things that ever mattered to me. I told him about Mary, about the dazzling magic of falling in love, about the strange way it ended and the permanent sense of loss I was stuck with. I spoke about my collision with learning up at Manchester; how I'd gone there with such certainty, and how the course had led me to question everything I ever knew, so that in the end my condition had been inverted and I couldn't be sure that *anything* was true the way it used to be. I told him about my first few years as a teacher; the complexity of the entrapment I felt within and around me: the homesickness, the pretence in the classroom of being respectable, of knowing true values, of certainty; the pretence in the staffroom of being normal, conservative, solvent, and keen on all those sick little sons and daughters of all those depressive, aggressive, *certain*, neurotic, complacent parents; the hours of pointless marking, carefully composing comments which I *knew* would be completely disregarded and which, even if read, would always be outshone by the pointless, arbitrary grade in the margin; the sense of panic in despising the good kids for whom I was so grateful; the absurdity of rooting for the rebels whose antics were such a colossal drag; the pathetic condition of only living, only actually being *alive* for six weeks in every year; the fake camaraderie; the egos; the jargon; the ludicrous position of actually welcoming a strike because it would enable me to catch up on my *work*; the endless sequence of empty Sundays poisoned by the knowledge of what day it would be tomorrow; the desperation so wild that when I finally surrendered I fled, not back home to southern safety, there to lick my wounds, but away to Mexico for what I hoped would be a desert, a tangible nothing of hotness and tired dust; the feeling that even *that* would probably be too much, that what I *really* needed was a long age amid Inca ruins, where only death was truly known, where a petrified imagination had postponed indefinitely the advent of circular motion.

I could almost hear music as I spoke of Mexico: a dark brooding sweep of gargantuan orchestral uplift seemed to gather and swell in my ears. I spoke of my cynical acceptance that I was merely engaged in exporting 'O' levels to English brats in exile; I made passing reference to my genteel English sensibility which was so shocked, at first, by the unashamed vulgarity of the natives, and so unwillingly too. It *was* only a passing reference though, because in Mexico City I did at least, and at last, find the heat and dust I had hoped for. And it was my extreme position, in this landscape of extremity, which gave birth at last to my vision: my final realisation that going away had been only a cleansing, a burning off of the straw and stubble of my existence, a stepping back from the present to see the full picture of my past, and I acknowledged consciously what a decade of emptiness had been mutely indicating all along. Past, present and future suddenly became irrelevant, no more important than a grade in the margin of an exercise book. I realised that *when* matters very little; it is *what* that really counts. And since other people's reality had proved to be as worthless as it was tenuous and corrupt, I resolved to create my own. I would stand. I would insist. I would make the world a happy place. It would be a world of my own making.

And I knew I had to go back for Mary. It was simple. I had to go back to the last point in my life where there had been something worth making a world *for*; and, incidentally, someone to make it *with*. I had to reclaim the garden from the wilderness.

I must have talked, uninterrupted, for the best part of an hour. Crispin's Day wasn't in it. Bellamy looked sad at first, then he looked worried; but as I kept on I saw him settle and begin to feel the spirit of what I was saying. By the end he was sitting back, relaxed and smiling at me, and I knew I had won him over.

BELLAMY

We argued it out for a while. He could tell I was serious because everything I said was good common sense. He didn't know what had happened to her in the last twelve years. He didn't know if she was *married* or what. The worst thing was, he just *assumed* she'd want to go away with him. He didn't seem to think about *her* life. But he said all that stuff didn't matter. Said I was missing the point.

Then he laid his trip on me like a ton of bricks. I mean, he started off at about three and after a while he looked set for a couple of days. Almost his whole life story. I don't know how long it took from beginning to end but I knew by the time he got to university I could say goodbye to the football.

I listened though, because really and truly I wanted to understand it.

Well, something hit him in Mexico. It wasn't a bandit, which is what I was expecting, it was more theoretical than anything. It amounted to the same thing though, because *I* reckon he had his *brain* stolen out there. When he got on to Coleridge and Wallace Stevens I just got lost.

But then I looked at him, and the thing that made me feel better about it was just the fact that it was still *him*. I mean, we'd been out a few times and everything, and I knew he hadn't *really* changed. He wasn't actually crazy. I was just glad to have him back, really.

So then I started thinking what the hell. All he really wanted me to do was ride out to the fens with him. I thought he'd need someone to buy him a beer when the girl told him to take a hike. Business was slow. I could take the camera. Nothing really to lose.

So I quietened down then. I just sat back and listened. He talked up a storm for another twenty minutes or so. It was almost like old times, when we used to go for coffee and talk all night. It made me feel good, actually, to have that old connection back.

At the end he said, "There. That's what I'm going for. Nothing less than saving the whole dang world. Now, either you're *on* the bus or you're *not* on the bus. So what do you say?"

I said, "Count me in. It's crazy, impossible, and it'll end in tears, but I'll do it."

He smacked a fist into his hand and stood grinning out the window saying, "Damn right. Damn right it's impossible. Damn right it is."

PERIODICAL

AN INTERVIEW WITH ROBIN WILLIAMSON

In conversation, as in performance and on record, Robin Williamson is a kind of magician, a wizard with words and music and always a twinkle in his eye. Sometimes he will supply no details at all: Where in Wales does he live? "*South* Wales." Did he read much as a child? "Yes." Sometimes vagueness edges you away from a topic. Scientology? "That was a long time ago." But his default setting is tirelessly enthusiastic warmth and extreme generosity with his time. A quality he finds in gospel bluesman Willie Johnson seems most apt for Williamson himself: "Heartfulness."

What stories, myths and legends have particular resonance for you?
Well actually all of them. From the simplest nursery tale like Jack and the Beanstalk, all the way up to stories like the Battle Of Moytura which is like almost the beginning of everything, the big stories and the little stories all have got some kind of meaning, which becomes apparent to certain people at certain times. A certain story can find you at the time in your life when you need that story.

In even the simplest sort of story there are certain key messages which emerge, and one of them is that LUCK is something which can be attracted. The stories seem to say that the qualities of generosity and humility attract luck, but arrogance, pride and meanness repel it.

Does that square with your experiences of life in the world?
Life in the world is to me some sort of miracle which I haven't the slightest idea how to quantify or talk about. It seems to me that Life itself is neither sacred nor profane, but what we can do is honour

the extraordinary majesty that is the universe and the inexplicable reality of being here in the first place. We can honour that certain degree of respect which we might as well call SANCTITY; that's something that humans can do to acknowledge the extraordinary MYSTERY of reality.

You once said that your songwriting was influenced by Jack Kerouac. People like Jack Kerouac and Charles Bukowski used to write in a very apparently spontaneous manner. They would let the words flow, and I loved that. I discovered William Blake via Kerouac. The notion of the inspired voice is a very BARDIC notion, and a very traditional notion in the Celtic heritage of say Wales and Ireland. The notion was that there was some kind of BARDIC SECRET, which had something to do with INSPIRATION and having a voice of POWER and PROPHECY. And prophecy was not just prediction, but saying something about what is.

Early on in particular I tried to write in a very free flowing way, but later, influenced by Dylan Thomas, I tried to use words in a very concrete way and pick words very carefully, and sometimes work on a song for quite a long time.

Was Dylan Thomas a big influence?
Yeah. On one hand somebody like him and on the other hand someone like Duncan Williamson, for completely different reasons. Duncan became a very good friend.

He's a traveller and storyteller who recently died. He used to call himself my honorary uncle because my second name is Duncan as well. He was quite well known in the storytelling field. I loved the way that he put large pieces of his life into his stories and I love the way that Dylan Thomas was a sculptor with words.

I wonder if you draw a distinction between things that you like and things that have influenced you?
Oddly enough, some of the people that I most admire I don't actually copy that much. For instance one of my great heroes is Blind Willie Johnson. What I love about him is his HEARTFULNESS. I myself will never be able to express that sort of emotion in that way but I can really relate to what he's feeling. And sometimes when you come to some crossroads or turning point in life, when everything falls apart and goes wrong, you find yourself leaning on the eternal truths in a variety of ways and that's when transformative experiences can really occur.

You are an honorary Chief Bard in the Order of Bards Ovates and Druids.
(Laughs)

How did this happen?
Somebody asked me! Philip Carr-Gomm I believe.

Did he explain why they wanted to honour you in this way?
Not as such. I assumed it had something to do with the words I'd said or the songs I'd sung. Lovely little ceremony on Primrose Hill.

Do you follow any specific religious practices?
I think the practice that's most important is to remember one's place in the order of things and to celebrate the privilege of consciousness.

Our planet is not acknowledged as a wonderful conscious entity and the universe itself being not only a series of forces and laws and numerical powers but also having an instructional force in it. The consciousness we possess is the key to plugging into that force. I think the universe desires to be understood and I think our consciousness is part of the universe coming into greater consciousness. We're deeply connected to each other, us and the universe, and that is the important practice, for me.

Is the universe a moral place?
It's an **INSTRUCTIONAL** place. It's a source of wisdom. It's the old thing about ask and you shall receive, knock and it shall be opened unto you, seek and ye shall find. My wife Bina and I once did a concert to celebrate the re-installation of a holy well in Penrhys. Long ago it was a famous holy well with a wonderful image that had formed itself in a tree, an image which resembled the mother and child. People travelled from all over Europe to go to this place which at that time in the middle ages was in a forest but the image was torn down in the dissolution of the monasteries, and the wondrous tree was burned. From that point the village declined. It ended up as a notoriously bad housing estate. Me and Bina went up there years ago and did a little concert as part of the celebration of the opening up of this holy well as a place of pilgrimage by the Catholic church, and it was just the most wonderful experience. Funnily enough, since opening up that well the village itself has got a new sense of self-esteem, which has been restored by restoring the well. Never underestimate the importance of powerful places if there is knowledge of this stuff. It's so sad if they are left to decay and not acknowledged, and that applies not only to places but also to the world itself.

Do you follow any specific rituals in your daily or seasonal observances?

Every night I light a candle. I stay in touch with the great creator. In the last 12 years or so I've been working a lot with my wife Bina, and what we've been trying to do is to celebrate the extraordinary fact of being alive, and the passing of the seasons in their order and we're drawing on different parts of folklore and how they reflect the turning year, but also drawing on different types of religious material and how they try to speak about the things that can't be spoken about, the things which are impossible to say, like why are we here, where are we going, all these questions which are not answerable. All the great religions try to talk about those things but there isn't an answer to any of them and it seems to me that the answer lies outside of all the great dogmas, and we find ourselves pretty much on the outskirts of most of the major clubs. However, that leaves us very firmly with the inexplicable wonder of things, and that's a great place to be.

You are a multi-faith person basically I think.

I think I would have to say so, although I don't adhere to any particular one.

With all the great religions so many things have gone wrong when they become dogmatic and sectarian. I think a high dose of tolerance is required at the moment in the world.

Do you still run courses and workshops?

Yes. Generally twice a year. They're on our website pigswhiskermusic.co.uk.

When did you take up the Celtic harp?
1980. I've been recently giving workshops in the harp. I think the harp is a wonderful instrument, it's a magical and ritual instrument. One of the three qualities of a gentleman in the old triads was to have a harp.

Do you have a quotation to guide you through life?
Thousands of them. One of them I particularly like is "From joy we are born, in joy we live; at death it is to joy that we return." That's from one of the Upanishads. What about this one: "The perfect has no self, the holy no merit, the wise no fame." Chuang Tsu, I believe.

The holy has no merit?
Yeah, there's no point in showing off about being so holy.

But is there any point in trying to be holy?
Well I think there's every point in trying to be holy but I'm just saying that merit is not the reason. (Laughs)

You're living this life. Do you think you've lived a previous life?
I think it's pretty likely, yeah.

And you think you might be back again?
All the things in nature seem to be so cyclical and seem to emerge one-into-another, I think that perhaps when one dies it's maybe like a drop of water falling into a sea or returning to a great All or else it could be that the spark of soul re-emerges as another spark

of soul in another incarnation, I just don't know really but I'm pretty sure that death is not kaput. I have to think about this quite a lot because at my age one thinks about death quite a lot!

The place me and Bina played in mid Wales was near Llandrindod Wells. It was on a tiny little road, and this is the extraordinary thing: in the sixties I used to live near Newport, Pembrokeshire and some of the guys that we lived with there had moved to a house not far from Llan Wells and [our gig] turned out to be on the same little road. The chances against it must have been millions to one to end up on that same little road; the Quaker meeting house wasn't even in use at that point, it had fallen into disrepair. And they were living on a farm further up the road.

Serendipity.
Yes there is such a thing. Coincidences.

People ascribe it to random chance but some of us aren't so sure.
It's definitely not random chance, and what's more, as soon as you firmly set your feet on some sort of path then a series of coincidences starts occurring to you and things that you need to know mysteriously and miraculously crop up. That seems to me to be an observable truth.

Yes, especially if it's the path that you should be on.
Yes the path that you should be on, that you know you've gone the right way, and then all of a sudden life starts laying itself on for you in some way, sometimes a lot more than you bargain for.

Have you observed that sometimes you encounter a bit of opposition early on as well?

Yes, you encounter quite a lot of opposition. Things that they used to call daemonic forces. In the Tree of Life in the Kabbal? Well that's of course absolutely fascinating stuff, and I did one workshop on the Paths and songs which relate to them, using songs as keys to open certain paths, between the terrestrial, Malkuth, and the spiritual, Tiferet.

SACRED SONGS PART THREE

'Peace To All Beings' by James Asher

Let's not beat about the you-know-what, 'Peace To All Beings' by James Asher is *new age* music. There are, at the very least, two problems with new age music: one is its apparent blandness, and the other is the artificial, frequently *synthesised* form that it often takes, typically produced on a keyboard making heavy use of effects rather than authentic musical instruments. 'Peace' is, I fear, largely guilty on the second count, and it could be found holding a bloodstained weapon at the crime-scene for the first accusation too, except that I feel it is unfair to label as bland a music that often actually *tries* to blend into the background. After all, no one criticises shamanic drum tracks for being repetitive and lacking musical development, so why complain if the hypnotic drones of Joe Peacenik and his Blissed-Out Drip-Hop Orchestra actually do send you to sleep? The point is, does it make you feel the way you want to feel? In James Asher's case the answer is a resounding yes.

In the wheel of the Celtic year, Lughnasadh is the season of greatest duality. We start our annual voyage in the dark days of Samhain, gaining energy in the resurgence of Imbolc and hitting our stride at Beltane, but Lammas brings both the climax and the beginning of decline; we gather the harvest and taste the fruit, but we also begin our journey back to darkness and the year's ending. At such a time it is appropriate to give thanks for all the goodness the year has brought, and to meditate on the cycle of life that brings us, we would hope, satisfaction, completion and rest. If your autumnal meditations follow this pattern, then 'Peace To All Beings' is the perfect accompaniment.

Musically, 'Peace' is a compound of standard new age ingredients. It sets up with a vibraphone sound and quickly fills it out with a soundwash that blends various keyboard and string effects. Within a few moments of the start the vibraphone has already slipped into a four-second loop that will be repeated unceasingly for *twenty long minutes*. How does Mr Asher sustain our interest with such entrenched material?

First, he builds a pattern of change using possibly the oldest spell in the musical grimoire, the separation of treble and bass. Picture two hands on the keyboard. The right hand is the vibraphone loop; it stays fixed in position, constantly repeating, while the *left* hand shifts the bass notes gradually down (and up again) in regular intervals, creating a variation on the basic chord at each step. It is a trick used in a thousand dance tracks of the 1980's, and it *always* works.

Asher also builds variety into the piece by adding a roster of woodwind, orchestral and other sound effects on a periodic basis, none of them outstaying their welcome and all of them combining to build atmosphere whilst weaving small threads of melody through the musical structure.

So far so fine, but there are three other aspects of 'Peace' which make it of special value for those who revere our Mother Earth.

The most fundamental element of beauty here is simply the actual *sound* of it. Asher has found the warmest, most uplifting, shimmering noise to capture the fullness of autumn's orchard and the happiness of the pagan heart. There is a stillness and calmness held in the slow, steady deployment of the sound that perfectly expresses that feeling of gratitude and rest found in Lughnasadh at its height. 'Peace' really does invite you to pause, reflect and give thanks for the blessings of the year in its final phase.

Another highlight is the introduction, halfway through the twelfth minute, of a very real-sounding and beautiful piano. It stays for less than a minute and does nothing spectacular, but it certainly lifts the heart and communicates joy in harmony with the spirit of the season.

But the cleverest aspect of this composition is the fact that it is written in a *minor* key. This means that, despite all the warmth, all the fulfilment, all the inherent happiness in the *tone* of the piece, there is always a hint of melancholy, always a slight mournfulness and feeling of loss somewhere below the surface. Thus James Asher's music embodies the duality of autumn mentioned earlier. The ripeness of fruition is also the end of the journey and the first sign of the death and decay that will eventually return us all to the Earth from which we came.

If you are seeking a soundtrack to your meditations on the joys and griefs of Lughnasadh, welcoming the gold of harvest time whilst providing a valediction to the beauty of autumn, 'Peace To All Beings' could be exactly what you need.

JOHN MORIARTY: CHRISTIAN VISIONARY

June 1st 2007 was the last day in the earthly life of John Moriarty. Those in the know mourned the loss of a man whose life quest took him through wide-ranging territory. Poetry, philosophy, academia, autobiography and horticulture are just a few of the things he excelled at but, for me at least, Moriarty is most closely associated with two things: his knowledge of myth and story, and his attempts to re-envision Christianity and restore at least some of its heart.

An astrologer once told me that Aquarian males are nearly always rare, outstanding individuals. Moriarty, born a farmer's son in County Kerry on February 2nd 1938, provides good evidence. His own mother once remarked that he "didn't even look like a fact of life."

Moriarty was a success in the academic world. He left University College, Dublin with a double-first in Philosophy and English Literature. After travelling in Europe he began postgraduate work at Leeds, tutoring undergraduates to help fund his studies there. Later he taught Literature at the University of Manitoba. After eight years of this, however, his dissatisfaction with academic life (and the call of his Celtic cultural heritage) got the better of him and he returned to Europe, eventually working as a gardener, first in England and then in Ireland.

In the mid 1980's Moriarty began appearing on RTE Radio1. His expressive voice and extensive cultural understanding made him a natural for the medium. His first book, *Dreamtime*, was published by Lilliput Press in 1994 and two years later came the first volume of his great trilogy, *Turtle Was Gone A Long Time*. Several other books followed, including part one of his acclaimed autobiography, *Nostos*. In 2002 he bought the land for Slina Firinne, a Christian educational project which has continued to develop since his death.

The main elements of John Moriarty's life include mythology, storytelling, ecology and philosophy, but woven through them all is a muscular and clear-eyed Christianity which tries to be both personal and universal, monastic and fully engaged in public cultural debate.

Turtle Was Gone A Long Time is certainly an ambitious work. Some very learned Pagan folk have suggested it is best to dip into it serendipitously rather than working through it from start to finish. They may be right, but personally I would recommend the more straightforward approach as I believe that will give you a better feel of its grand scale and rhetorical momentum. What follows is not exactly a critical analysis or review of it. I simply offer this general survey of the book in the hope that I might encourage you to seek it out and explore it for yourself.

The first, towering aspect of *Turtle* is Moriarty's writing style. Rather like Louis Armstrong or Tom Waits, Moriarty is one of those artists whose voice turns almost everything he does into a spell or charm. He enthrals you, and his written expression is so personable and musical that he could, I believe, write a description of paint drying that would keep you beguiled to the very last syllable.

Moriarty's is a very Irish voice. It is also a poet's voice. Most of all it is the voice of a storyteller. This affects the structure as well as the tone of the book. For all its weight and mighty ambition, the trilogy meanders, circles and repeats in a conversational way that takes you in loops of magnificent grandeur and modest, gentle anecdote. Here are some highlights from along the way:

VOLUME ONE: CROSSING THE KEDRON
Moriarty lays the groundwork of his epic vision here, building from small stories towards the unified vision that is to come.

Close to the start he recounts a short colonial tale that ends with the moral, "We have moved so far, so fast, that now we must sit here and wait till our souls catch up." He takes us into the furthest deeps of ground level, asserting, "Until we have learned to stand deep in the earth we shouldn't even think of setting foot on the moon."

He connects the Earth and the spiritual, and combats a wrong turn made in the twentieth century: "Freud talked about repressed sexuality. He didn't talk about repressed soul. Ignored soul. Excluded soul is the great calamity of our age."

A hundred pages in he delivers a central idea he will thread through the book: "Putting it brutally, psyche is the blind, not the window." Later, his own recollection of a child witnessing the birth of a cow gives rise to a deep and charming parable showing Moriarty's magical storytelling art. Such autobiographical material is woven through the rest of the book, sharing space with Hindu, Buddhist, Christian, Aboriginal and American traditions to set up a vision of a faith that is inclusive rather than exclusive, where tolerance and mutual respect are not just aspects of religious practice, they *are* the practice.

VOLUME TWO: HORSEHEAD NEBULA NEIGHING

This is where Moriarty issues his challenge to Christianity, asking when it will be "big enough for Jesus," when will it live up to the precepts of its originator? It is like an old-fashioned call for revival, but on a much grander and more profound scale than most orthodox Christians are likely to recognise. Moriarty describes it as "our space journey to the Earth," and "the only space journey worth embarking on. At the end of it we will see Earth as Buddh Gaia and the universe as a Bodhi tree."

Moriarty is fully into his stride in this volume, blending the anecdotal and the universal, the fragments and the entire, and he weaves them together with all the drama, pathos, humour and warmth that a true, healing magician can wield. There is hardly a page that does not spark and enlighten the worlds of faith, history and humanity.

VOLUME THREE: ANACONDA CANOE

The final part of Moriarty's campaign contains some of the strongest and weakest pages. His attempts to communicate the big picture lurch disappointingly into spirit-babble just near the end, citing "darkness beyond light" and "vision through loss of sight." But there is still plenty of valuable stuff here. The introduction features a powerhouse apologia synthesising a range of poets and making claims for Christianity's ability to meet the needs of this age of Darwin, mammon and secular self-destruction. He continues to weave inspirational stories from wide-ranging traditions through the argument, and the sense of dramatic momentum is at its highest in these pages where Melville meets *Elvira Madigan* meets a Blackfoot Indian buffalo story.

For those Pagans who feel they have little time for a Christian mystic's viewpoint, John Moriarty is an excellent point from which to embark on an exploration.

TEACHERING MORE BETTERER

Jeremy Hunt's dismissive response to NHS staff concerns last week served only to confirm my long-held suspicions about him. His high-handed approach carries the smug complacency of privilege coupled with the dogmatic ignorance of a rigidly closed mind.

Mr Hunt is likely to remain famous long after his demise, as a piece of rhyming slang. Even that annoys me. I remember the gleeful sniggering when James Naughtie got his consonants in a tangle introducing Mr Hunt on the radio. Oh listen, everyone, I can't even do the one simple thing I'm paid to do without fouling up. And I used a rude word. Ha bloody ha.

Mr Hunt was at that time the Culture Secretary, a worthwhile job albeit not as life-and-death crucial as his current post. He was pretty useless at it, but that did not prevent his appointment as Health Secretary a while later. Such is the paucity of talent at Mr Cameron's disposal.

Mr Hunt was educated (I use the term advisedly) at Charterhouse School and Oxford University. Well, look it up if you don't believe me. We have a very strange concept of education in Britain; so strange in fact that it has become possible for Nicky Morgan to be put in charge of it.

Mrs Morgan, who is also an Oxford graduate (staggering, I know, but true), looks and behaves like a Ragdolly Anna puppet attempting, with all the lame gusto she can summon, to sound confident and knowledgeable about government policy five minutes after it has been formulated and foisted on her, and a couple of months before it will be at least partially rescinded.

Mr Hunt and Mrs Morgan, and several others in Mr Cameron's team, are clumsy and inept. It's so depressingly obvious: they're just not bright enough; they're not up to the job; should never have been considered, much less appointed.

In my final few years as a teacher my union invariably got stroppy with the then Education Secretary, Michael Gove. It's true that Mr Gove's judgement was not always coupled with wisdom and perspective, but I liked him. I used to enjoy his appearances on BBC TV's 'Question Time' because you could see very clearly that he was not afraid of thinking aloud, right there, live, in front of the cameras and a critical public. That is what a proper education can do for you, if you're lucky enough to get one.

Sadly, it does seem to be a matter of luck. It is certainly not privilege. The lamentable Mr Hunt proves this, as do many others in both main parties. Nor does it depend on academy status, however keenly the carpetbaggers of educational exploitation might wish it did.

Last week also witnessed a gratuitous 'strike' by primary school children, withdrawn by their parents complaining of stressful tests. In my experience schoolchildren actually like tests, finding them useful, informative and good discipline. What they don't like is a lack of point and structure in their school activities. They get enough of that at home.

I would like to see Education taken completely away from the swings and lurches of politics. We have a divide in this country between those who champion market forces and those who seek to value all cultural choices equally. The pc dogmatists want us all to wallow, or drown, in our own free choice of mudhole; the free enterprisers believe that whatever rises to the top is the best, and they are not much concerned whether it is the cream or the scum. Both include the word 'free' in their rhetoric; neither of them actually means it. Education is much too important to be put under the control of these posturing rabble-rousers. We need an education system with values that transcend the faddish and reactionary altogether.

Have you ever noticed that the people who sneer most loudly at the 'nanny state' are the ones most likely to have actually had a nanny in their younger days? They have absorbed the benefits of having a dedicated guardian, guide and teacher, and they take those benefits for granted; they think the rest of our 3D society (deprived, depressed and depraved) should probably be punished for having such a poor start in life anyway.

Well, I am a strong advocate of the nanny state, especially for the young, impressionable and vulnerable types who often attend (albeit reluctantly) our educational establishments. I believe if the state does not nanny the little children, someone or something else will.

When I was a school student myself, in the 1960's, the timetable included 'Religious *Instruction*' and 'Physical *Training*'. Such terms indicated a consciousness, an attitude, that sought to equip young people with a set of values and principles that might guide them through every trial of life.

There is instruction and training today, but it focuses on footling areas where terms like adverbial conjunction are seen as important enough to be tested.

I am not, of course, arguing that we should put 'Religious Instruction' back on the timetable. But we should be training our children to think, learn and behave in ways that will steer them through their entire lives, not just the next set of tests or the current crop of jobs.

When I was twelve I injured my left hand. For several months, while the hand was healing, I had to adopt a new way of dressing, putting my left hand into its sleeve first, to protect it from further damage. Half a century later I *still* put my left hand in first when dressing. I was trained to do it that way at an impressionable age, and it has stuck for life. That is not an important thing to learn at the age of twelve; let educators, elders and wise people decide what is. And let us please keep posturing politicians and ignorant schoolchildren out of the decision-making process.

You will say the previous paragraph is anecdotal evidence; it is not supported by statistical evidence and the demands of the modern market place. But I believe we should be guided by moral judgement and long-term values; they will at least stand a chance of leading us to paradise. Short-term values, stats and the pressures of commerce will lead us to places like Bhopal.

HOW TO PLAY BOMB THE GLIDER

BOMB THE GLIDER was originally called Bomb The Frisbee, but I am steering away from any potential copyright problems and keeping it as generic as possible. Frisbee is perhaps like Hoover and Thermos in the UK: the brand name has become adopted as the name of the product itself. In the UK it would not be considered contradictory to say that you have just bought a Dyson hoover to replace the old Electrolux hoover that finally conked out after decades of use. So my immediate task is to make clear that this game uses what I will call a glider, meaning a flying disc of the kind that many people refer to as a frisbee.

OBJECT OF THE GAME:
- To reach a total of 11 (eleven) points and/or to help your opponent(s) do the same.
- To exercise self-interest and generosity together.
- To observe the results.

EQUIPMENT:
- One glider, or flying disc of the kind often referred to here in the UK as a 'frisbee'.
- One tennis ball for each person playing.

PLAYING SURFACE:
- The ideal is a flat, level, grassy area of approximately 50 yards square or more.
- The vital elements are: sufficient space (on the ground and overhead) for wayward throws to be retrieved, and a reasonably

soft landing for those who stumble, trip, leap and dive.
- But almost *any* surface may be suitable, including (especially if wheelchairs are involved) a hard paved area.

THE INSTRUCTIONS THAT FOLLOW are for the standard model, two-person form of the game. If there are more players, simply divide into two teams. You will need an extra tennis ball for each added player.

For ease of reference the two sides will be labelled throwers and bombers. While these terms are used here in fixed form it must be remembered that, with each turn of the game, the sides switch from throwing to bombing.

HERE IS WHAT HAPPENS IN A SINGLE TURN OF THE GAME:

STAGE ONE: THROWING
- The thrower sends the glider towards and above the bomber.
- The aim is to set the glider hovering/gliding above the bomber at a height that makes hitting it a challenge but reasonably achievable.
- The criterion at this point is very simple: if the bomber actually throws the tennis ball, s/he is accepting the glider as a reasonable target; if s/he holds on to the tennis ball, the glider is retrieved and returned to the thrower for another attempt.

STAGE TWO: BOMBING
- The bomber throws the tennis ball up at the glider.
- If the ball misses the glider, that is the end of the turn.
- If the ball hits the glider while it is in flight, the glider has been

bombed and the turn goes into recovery mode.
- Once the glider reaches the ground the ball can no longer be thrown at it.
- The ball must not be touching the thrower at the moment it hits the glider.
- Throwing style is a matter of individual choice, but most players find under-arm to be the most effective.

STAGE THREE: RECOVERY
- As soon as the ball hits the glider, *both sides* go into recovery mode.
- Every player close enough attempts to catch the ball and/or the glider before they reach the ground.

SCORING POINTS:
- The bomber who hits the glider with the ball scores one point.
- An additional point is scored *for the bomber* by any player who catches the ball and/or the glider before they reach the ground.
- Points are only scored if the glider is actually bombed. You should still try to catch a missed glider or wayward ball, but only as an act of sociable co-operation.

CONTINUING:
- Once recovery has concluded the sides switch roles to go through the three stages again.

CONCLUSION:
- Turns continue until one side reaches the winning total of eleven points.
- It might be thought that the side taking their turn first may

have a better chance of reaching the winning total first also, but experience has shown that successful bombing does not occur frequently enough for any significant advantage to obtain.

FINER DETAILS:

In the standard two-person game there will be a maximum of 3 (three) points achievable from any one turn. In team games it is possible that more than one ball will be caught, and it is also at least conceivable that more than one ball will hit the glider. *All balls that actually bomb the glider may be caught* to secure points for the bombing side. In practice, of course, this is all so unlikely that it hardly warrants further pursuit, but there is potential for confusion and uncertainty in team games where, for example, a ball that is caught may not be the ball that actually bombed the glider. In all such situations the players must contribute accurate, truthful information regardless of self-interest. A good guiding principle can be borrowed from football refereeing where, if you did not actually see a foul committed, you cannot award a penalty kick no matter what the balance of probability may be. Likewise, if you do not KNOW that this is the ball that hit the glider, you cannot score a point by the catching of it.

CHEATING (IN GENERAL)

In any game that *is* just a game and not a business or industrial racket, cheating should be bootless and unattractive. It may be hoped that where the *object of the game* is to help your opponent, cheating may be obviated. Ego, inadequacy and mental unwellness, however, can subvert almost any high-minded intention.

The analogy of music may help here. Show-offs distract attention from the song. We notice and admire the virtuosos and soloists, but there is a danger that they will reduce the emotional and intellectual payload of the composition. The best musicians have the discipline to do all their work *in the service of the song*. The same applies to Bomb The Glider: it's the *game* that matters most, and the players work to serve the game. Bill Shankly famously observed of football, "Some people think it's a matter of life and death, but it's a lot more important than that." It's such a funny remark that we don't always notice how wise it is too.

MISSION

It is one thing to play a game with levity and generosity, but please don't neglect the subversive potential here.

In the past we have seen professional cricket and tennis sell their souls (and every square inch of their clothing) for squalid cash, trampling the principle of respect for the fallible umpire in the process.

Put simply, it's no good unless you spread it around. If you find any value or pleasure in Bomb The Glider, you are urged to play it as often and with as many people as you are able, especially with children.

SONG

(The Ballad Of) JUSTIN CASE

Take a look at that skateboard freak.
What a freakin' disgrace.
He's got athlete's foot and, it looks like,
He's got athlete's face.
And just in case he bumps into you accidentally
You'd better come home with me.

And watch out for that puppy dog skipping round the park.
He'll be chasing those pigeons down until after dark.
And just in case he scares you, baby, barking up that tree,
You'd better come home with me

Where I can keep you well protected (if you're on your own).
If you want we can get connected. Who needs a freakin' phone?

I feel obliged to warn you, babe, that this is a busy road.
If there's a gas main under it, it just might explode
And those power cables carry electricity
So you'd better come home with me.

That's right, come on home with me, baby.
Take care on this busy road now.
Watch out, don't fall. Careful, don't trip.
I think you'd better hold my hand.
Did I mention that I'm single?

We could cook some kind of dinner and play a stupid game.
I could let you be the winner. You'll be glad you came.

You see that old age pensioner with the long grey beard?
I don't want to scare you but he's acting kind of weird
And, just in case he's a psycho killer about to go on a spree,
You'd better come home with me.

THE ELYSIAN FIELDS

Only love can find your space.
I can see the heartbreak written in your face grown now,
And if you're wondering where can it be today,
You are standing inside to say it.
Oh, lonely, heartbroken, almost every dream is turned about
But don't you worry, we can work it out.

We'll only ever change the world one heartbeat at a time;
Each broken-hearted boy and girl all standing in a line and broken-hearted.

On the jewelled carriageway, signs in procession precision;
And if you can be carried today you can make your decision.
They will open up before your eyes.
See the glistening of oceans, kiss the skies.
Hear the players, hear the singers, hear the voices in the air.
I will see you there.

One day we'll get to understand. One day we'll get to fly
Like seagulls over sparkling sands, and never have to cry,
Broken-hearted, lonely.

Go, go and fly back home. Don't be afraid of being alone.
We will never leave you crying in the rain. We'll see you smile again.

Oh, lonely, heartbroken, almost every dream is turned about
But don't you worry, we can work it out

We'll wipe all of those tears away, begin amazingly
To redeem us to a brighter day. We'll never have to be
Broken-hearted, lonely, broken-hearted…

FROM HERE ON IN TO ENGLAND

Over again, over again, I just don't know what to do.
Oh, how it drains, oh, how it pains when true love is vicious to you

And she looks in your eyes, she's telling you lies
Dressed in compassion with long heavy sighs
And not even a trace of guilt or disgrace,
Wondering how you can take it at face value.

Over again, over and then there'll be no more tears to be cried.
My heart won't ache, my heart won't break 'cause yesterday evening it died.

ONCE AND FUTURE KING

I was told when I was younger,
And I still believe it's true,
If you treat a person kindly then he might be kind to you.

Could the lesson be more simple?
Will the learning never end?
If you bomb a person's homeland he will never be your friend.

Now we hear the children crying when we long to hear them sing,
And the call is out to Arthur, the once and future king.

In the halls of exposition you can hear the empty sound
Of a power with no glory standing tall on shaky ground.
When your leader has no wisdom and your hope has all but died,
Hearing tales of brave adventure can rebuild your broken pride.

Now we see the children starving in our endless banqueting
And the call is out to Arthur, the once and future king.

POISON ROAD

I have seen the changes coming,
I have felt the chill wind blow.
I have felt that cold so numbing.
I have seen the road we have to go.
When the people break together they will feel a cold hard rain,
And the promise in this weather only speaks of loss and pain.

Now this road was once so pretty we would ride to town in joy,
But the darkness in the city steals the soul of ev'ry happy boy.
Now they break the spines of children on McHollywood and Vine.
Well that road is paved with poison and it never shall be mine.

They run all over the land as if it was theirs.
Nobody understands, nobody cares.
Oh, woe.
Oh no.

Now the sky turns black with money as the earth is bought and sold,
And the lawyers think it's funny so they claim the copyright control,
And you can tell the evil kingdom by the man we all detest:
He attacks the land of freedom and he was funded by the West.

THE FIRE THIS TIME

Out in the East they're burning the sky away,
Choking in Asia under a dark brown haze.
Caught in a horror story,
No one will say we're sorry and start again at the end.
Out to the West we're wanting the world to end,
Gas in the car and screaming around the bend.
Gone in a blaze of glory,
No one will say we're sorry and start again at the end,
So the fire burns as the wheel turns round.

Leave the city hell for leather.
See the tower fall and shatter.
Leave the city.
Leave for ever.
Take the open field and scatter.

Down in the South we're melting the ice away.
Don't want to get a cold summer holiday.
Hogging the territory,
No one will say we're sorry and start again at the end.
So the fire burns as the wheel turns round.

Leave the city,
Leave for ever.
Take the open field and scatter.

Leave the city.
Leave together.
What it offers doesn't matter.

GREENWOOD RIDE

Riding through the greenwood tonight.
Riding for the torches bright.
Riding through the dark,
Running for the light,
Riding through the greenwood tonight.

Questing over sacred ground.
Questing for the Table Round.
Stories for to tell,
Ations for to found,
Questing over sacred ground.

Where rests the grail?
There must I ride,
Sword from my lady at my side.
Here runs the path.
Where does it lead?
Horse from tomorrow, be my steed tonight.

Riding through the dark,
I hope I'll be all right,
Riding through the greenwood tonight.

TRUE LOVE ALWAYS

Time will wake you up with gentle warning,
Now you are a person fully grown,
Echoing that first fateful morning
When you pulled the sword out of the stone.

And it's true,
Reaching out can pull you through.
Yes, and I know when it's there,
Burdened down with ragged care now,
That this is true love always.

Faithful hearts will understand
That this is true love always for the welfare of the land.

Turning once again with the seasons,
Time will bring you round to autumn gold.
Merlin calls you, deep under reason,
Hidden in the stories you've been told.

And it's all true,
Broken hearts will sing to you.
Yes, and I know when it's there,
Burdened down with ragged care now,
That this is true love always.

Cause we'll be riding out soon.
The tide is turning now,
You can see the signs in the sky.
And even in the darkness, I've seen that serpent star;
Even heard an eagle's cry,
And this is true love always.

STAND BY YOU

Sing love's song.
Nothing can deny me.
This world will change no matter what we do.
Nothing's wrong if you are standing by me.
I'll stand by you.

In the winter frost that was everywhere around me,
In the howling wind I had to struggle through,
I was not lost, but still you came and found me.
I'll stand by you.

See the earth in springtime:
The blossom has to fall;
That's her call.
And when the morning comes,
The birds just have to sing.
That's their thing.

I will try to save your heart from sorrow.
I give my word, I always will be true.
Don't you cry. Whatever comes tomorrow,
I'll stand by you.

ALWAYS AND EVEN SO

The journey home is freighted with danger.
Whose woods these are I think I know.
They led the steps of the doe-eyed stranger
To lift the curse of the Dolorous Blow.
My sister's heart took flight with the feeling
That compassion and love must always prevail.
This stricken land needs the same kind of healing
For the power and grace to capture the Grail.
What's the story you've been told?
Death and glory? You're gonna have to hold your head up.

This modern world is disintegrating.
Do what you can to brighten the sky.
Sometimes the tree spends all winter waiting
Just to be kissed by the butterfly.
It's plain to see by the change in the weather
On a planet of anger breaking apart,
The time has come to rebuild it together
With the weapons of healing here in your heart.
Like the maiden, the brave and the bold,
Heavy laden still, you have got to hold your head up.

And out on the edge of tomorrow, Earth is turning cold.
I don't know if, under the sorrow, a hero's heart can hold.
Hold your heart up too.

I've known the heat of the battle and the hunting hound.
Mother, I hear the Earth's death rattle.
What the hell's that sound?

Before you break from ancient tradition,
Be sure there's somewhere better to go
Or you will find the human condition
Will pull you down to the dragons below.
Open your heart and speak when you hear it.
There's a power inside you waiting to rise,
And Mother Earth will be seen in the spirit
And the fire that's sparking out of your eyes.
It's the season of autumn and gold.
That's the reason you're gonna have to hold your head up.
Hold your heart up too.

Whose woods these are I think you know.

THE CROW ROAD

There's a high and lonesome road of long ago.
It is taken by the raven and the crow.
Crow, he flies so straight and true, but he's disappeared from view
And if you ask me Where's the crow gone? I don't know.

There's a big blue open heaven up above.
It was put there by your Mother in her love,
But it's burning 'cause, you see, in our struggles to be free,
She's the last one we've had time for thinking of.

Don't you cry now 'cause the war will soon be over now. I'm sure
I don't need to say much more. It's on the run.

Now I'm going back to where I first begun.
'Cause you've got to face the damage you have done,
And I'll do it if I dare. And I hope to see you there.
Brother, don't you wonder where I've gone.

THE SLEEPING LORD

ONE
We are riding across the plains:
Riders, guiding the horses' reins,
Bent on healing the hearts that break.
Sleeping Lord, it's time to wake.

Banners flying in a cloudy sky,
Ravens crying, identify
Hearts of fire with a stand to make.
Sleeping Lord, it's time to wake.

Why can't we love the Earth,
Cherish her ways?
It's eyes on fire,
It's hearts of ache instead.
The battle spills all over time and space.

Modern rulers are in disguise.
They try to fool us with what are lies.
It's night time now but, come daybreak,
Sleeping Lord …

TWO
We are riding across the plains,
Merlin guiding the horses' reins,
Bent on healing the hearts that break,
Doing good for goodness' sake.

Sleeping Lord, it's time to wake.
Wake!

LOOKING TO FIND LAND

For all the time in the world
I was sailing on a foreign sea with the steerage in my hand.
Oh, and ever more impatiently I was looking to find land.

I was looking to find land,
Cold and lonely from the start.
Oh, but now, when you take my hand,
I finally understand
How you hold me to your heart
And show me how this love of ours is true

For all the time in the world.

Searching oceans of uncertainty for a place to make my stand,
Oh, until you came and rescued me, I was looking to find land.

LEESWOOD BLUES

In the sun-baked desert out in Africa, how much sand is there?
If the universe is still expanding, how much room to spare?
When a mother sees her newborn baby, how much does she care?
I don't know.

In the frozen Arctic wilderness, how much ice and snow?
If a man learned all about everything, how much would he know?
How much swimming does a dolphin do in the deep below?
I don't know,

But that's how much you mean to me.
That's how much I care:
Just as much as breathing needs air.

How much water in the ocean, and how much does it weigh?
If a man kept talking for eternity, how much would he say?
And just how happy are the children when they're going out to play?
I don't know.

How much beating of the swallows' wings as they gather in the sky?
How much growing in a redwood tree as centuries go by?
And if you told me you were leaving me, how much would I cry?
I don't know,

But that's how much you mean to me.
That's how much I care:
Just as much as breathing needs air.

THE OLDEST WAR

Morning, raining, but I don't care, 'cause she's there,
Living near me; that's enough. I'm in love again.

Learning slowly the sweet misty pain once again,
Wounding, healing, take a hold. It's the oldest war.

Take warning. Take cover.
You've been so very wrong before
And you can't afford to be hurt that badly any more.

Morning.

YOUR KARMA RAN OVER MY DOGMA

Caught myself looking in the mirror.
Noticed you weren't standing there behind.
I woke up this morning with a headache,
Turn around, and look at what I find:
You took me by surprise you up and left me.
I must have missed the writing on the wall.
You took up so much time when you were with me
But since you left me, girl, you take it all.

And, baby, since you left, you take all my time up.
I don't get a minute to myself.
You ain't even give me time to climb up
To my old familiar place up on the shelf.

All the people that we used to see together,
They don't come to see me anymore.
They understand I've been severely wounded
In the latest battle of the oldest war.
I'm constantly in revery and thinking,
And my company is never any fun.
And the only time they all came round to see me
Was when I went and bought myself a gun

BLOODY RED BLUES

Woke up this mornin' with the blues all in my head.
Woke up this mornin', Lord, I wished that I was dead.
When I woke up this mornin' I was lyin' in bed.

Ain't no way you're gonna lose these blood red blues.

Well I woke up this mornin', I was feelin' so down.
When I woke up this mornin', man, the blood was all around
From that menstruatin' woman underneath my eiderdown.

Ain't no way you're gonna lose these blood red blues.

THIS BELEAGUERED FOUNDATION

He wasn't born with every kind of privilege
But still he had the guts to get it on.
He used to think he'd always be a winner.
He was wrong.

He heard the books and read the propaganda.
His back was weak but oh, his heart was strong.
He never thought he'd ever turn to Jesus.
He was wrong.

He was wrong, wrong, wrong.
He was wrong, wrong, wrong.
He was wrong, wrong, wrong.
He was wrong.

People used to talk to him in slogans,
And in the end they carried him along.
He used to think he'd stay that young forever.
He was wrong.

He'd go to see his girlfriend in the evenings.
He knew they had a love so real and strong.
He never thought she'd ever go and leave him.

(GIVE ME) YOUR WINNING SMILE

Well, I'm looking at you, babe, a walking down the street,
Snapping your fingers and shuffling your feet.
And I'm lookin' at you, babe, and ooh, you're lookin' fine.
Lookin' at you, babe, about to lose my mind.

So turn your radio on.
Before you know it the holiday's gone.
But summer's here so just come on
And give me your winning smile.
There is paradise and heaven in your eyes.
I could talk all night to you.

We've been going steady for long enough to know
That, given a chance our love will surely grow.
And I'm sorry I made you cry the other night.
Believe in me, baby, I never want to fight.

Oh, baby, what can I say?
I fall to pieces when you're away.
I need to have you back to stay
So give me your winning smile.

Ooh, baby I love you.
Ooh, darlin' I really do.

BROKEN IN LOVE

This feeling deep inside of me is something I can't hide.
You see, basically, I'm a simple man.
I've got a little common sense, and not much more intelligence.
I guess I'm dense. I do the best I can.

And now a feeling's coming through, dedicated all to you,
'Cause that is who I am thinking of.
And even now I realise it never could be otherwise.
It's no surprise to find it hurts to love.

Do you see? Do you understand?
Honey, I'm a broken man.
All men are broken in love.
Such a happy pain inside
Such a dark and crazy ride.
All men are broken in love,
Creaking under the strain.

If I can find a better way to hold your hand, I will do it.
If I can.

REBELLION IN HEAVEN
(a song in three voices)

ONE
Talking in abstract terms about suffering.
Still I've hardly seen exactly what I mean.
It's easier to brush away the pain.
Somehow they'll get by.
I won't really have to try.

Still all over the world little children die.
In my cosy home I've got two little kids of my own.
I don't know what I'd do if anything happened to them.
Still the power hides out of Jesus in the sky.

TWO
Our captors mean so well for us, I couldn't lay them blame
But still it's true that me and you have suffered just the same.
And argument is useless. You know they'd never choose
To give us back our love and turn us loose,

But we'll find a way out of this mess some day, baby, you and I.
We'll slip out past the palace guard and down the steps and fly
On a tangent left of centre and right of questions why
We're not going to let the children die.

We'll glide across the moonlit lawns and underneath the trees.
Threatened by the jangle, we'll prob'ly dump the keys,
And the jailer's bound to find them, and it's bound to make him sore
To find out we don't need them anymore.

THREE
You never cared about me. You never gave a damn.
And there you go, and here I am.

LYRIC GREEN

In good brown fields the ploughmen stand
Or walk with horses to and fro,
And as they stride across the land
They hardly dream what soon shall grow.

The broken soil is turned and milled
By men and weather, work and wear
For Earth's good men are highly skilled
And work a partnership of care.

When spring returns the colours change
And good green fields from brown uprise,
And still we find it wondrous strange
Our earth still turns so warm and wise.

The sun burns dry the golden corn
And fills with gold the hands of men
So this good grain can be reborn
When Earth's great circle turns again.

But some would make the seeds their own
And seek to harvest only gold.
They love not all the good that's grown
And all their hearts are icy cold.

I look into the future now
And hear our starving children cry.
If men won't share this earth somehow,
The world we love shall surely die.

ECLIPSE

It's hopeless, you always knew it.
Never gonna bring back the disappeared.
All this campaigning will never do it.
You hold the night time to cover your fear

And then daylight bleeds into the skyline
And gently makes the shadows fly.
Daylight creeps over the horizon
And scares your heart into one more try.

No candle to expose the heartless.
No moon to signal the turning years.
Eclipsed now, on the edge of darkness,
You hold the night time to muffle your tears

And then daylight bleeds into the skyline
And gently makes the shadows fly.
Daylight creeps over the horizon
And scares your heart into one more try.

WILLINGHAM GIRLS

I've been all around this county
Lookin' for to find me a girl
One who smiles all the while
And puts your head in a whirl.
I've finally found me a place, my friend, and I'll tell you where I am.
You'll find me living in a village by the name of Willingham.

Willingham girls are the best in the county,
Willingham girls, they sure are sweet.
Willingham girls, they drive me crazy,
Always knocking me off my feet.
Willingham girls, they're so dang beautiful.
They're the kind of girls that I like to meet.
Willingham girls are the best in the county.
Willingham girls just can't be beat.

Now, Cambridge girls got beauty,
And Bottisham girls are kind,
And man, them girls from Madingley,
They pretty near blow your mind.
Well, I loved me a girl from Girton
But she broke my heart in two,
And it cost me two years' crying
But Willingham pulled me through.

BIZARRO WORLD

All the homeless people freezing by the fire
They just need a place to go
A politician is a special kind of liar
Paid for what he doesn't know

All the Burghermeisters preaching liberation
Building jails to keep us free
While the future that they're promising the nation
Isn't what it used to be

And there's nothing they can say for the good
But they'll say it anyway or they would if they could

All the children dehydrating by the river
They're just queueing up to die
They don't know that we're just balancing the figures
All day long I hear them cry

All the students practise sleeping on a wire
In a pool of neon light
Digging holes so they can stand a little higher
While they're running from the fight

And there's nothing they can do for the good
They don't lend a hand to you but they would if they could

And they're laughing all the while at the good
And you never see them smile but they would if they could

SONG FOR BERNADETTE

I will try to keep this simple;
No need to twist it all around.
I do not claim to be a wise man
But here's some wisdom I have found.
Nothing much in life is certain
But this one statement is true:
If I know anything
I know that I love you.

FIELDS THEY LOVED

Plugging in and switching on my lead.
Playing till my fingers start to bleed.
Rock 'n' roll is getting out of hand,
And me, I'm in a rock 'n' roll band.

Mog and Skiff are playing drums like hell
And the bass is coming over well
But the lead guitar's the poorest in the land
And me, I'm in a rock 'n' roll band.

If I want to I could ride a way,
Ride away and get it on.
If I want to I could ride away,
Ride away, ride away. Oh, no.

Oh, but Mog and Skiff are playing drums like hell
And the bass is coming over well
But the lead guitar's the poorest in the land.
My girl's around the block,
She's staring at the clock,
And me, I'm in a rock 'n' roll band.

NIGHT SONG IN SHERWOOD

Heard it on the wind tonight,
Scary in the wood:
No one's ready for this fight,
Nothing's any good.

Hearts of hurt and sorrow,
Turn and face tomorrow

Cause we're never going to build a better land
Running from the things we've seen
In England's green.

MARIAN'S FAREWELL

There's been just a little too much pain today for me,
Saying a last farewell to my remaining family.
I went looking for some answers
But only questions came.
I'm leaving my home.
I'm fed up with this game.

So I'm going back to Sherwood in the morning.
I don't care what anybody says.
Sherwood people never use a crossbow,
Sherwood people play it as it lays.
I've had enough of power crazy people
And those who take advantage of the poor.
Ignorance is doing all the talking these days
And I don't want to come here any more.

Skirting the river road past the ancient bridleway,
Only the few who know find the secret hideaway
Where heroes go to hiding
From the cowards in command
And ordinary people need a helping hand.

So I'm going back to Sherwood in the morning.

WEDDING SONG

The CHORUS is sung by the entire congregation; it starts the song and is sung again after each stanza. Stanzas may be sung by one or both spouses, shared or divided as preferred, thus allowing the song to be the ceremony itself if that is acceptable to those involved.

If 'for his bride' is not an apt expression in stanza three, the phrase 'open eyed' may be substituted.

CHORUS
    Love come down, love come down
    Bless us all around
    Make one life abound
    Out of two
    Love come down, love come down
    Bless us all around
    Keep the love we've found
    Always true

    One here knows you well
    Knows you to be good
    No one ever could
    Take your place
    One here knows your love
    Not in any doubt
    Sees it shining out
    Of your face

One here knows the way
Knows it to be true
Bound to only you
All my days
One here takes your heart
Takes your loving hand
By your side to stand
For always

One here faithfully
Takes you for his bride
Standing by your side
Every day
One here promises
Ever to be true
Always loving you
Come what may